Grassic Gibbon

and his World

Peter Whitfield

D1224798

ABERDEEN JOURNALS LTD

Published by Aberdeen Journals Ltd 1994
© Peter Whitfield

ISBN. 0 9510642 66

Typeset by EMS Phototypesetting, Berwick upon Tweed
in 11/14 point Baskerville

Printed by Kyodo Printing Co.

Contents

Rebecca Middleton (Ray Mitchell)

We shall not cease from exploration
And the end of all our exploring
Will be to arrive where we started
And know the place for the first time.
Through the unknown, remembered gate
When the last of earth left to discover
Is that which was the beginning;
At the source of the longest river
The voice of the hidden waterfall
And the children in the apple-tree
Not known, because not looked for
But heard, half-heard, in the stillness
Between two waves of the sea.

T. S. Eliot: *Little Gidding*

Preface

The only possible reason for writing about Lewis Grassic Gibbon is out of admiration for his work. *A Scots Quair* is one of those books which remain with the reader for life, and to which he constantly returns, while other more famous literary masterpieces weigh down the bookshelves but are never re-opened.

Many people will think that the *Quair* is such a clear, powerful book that commentaries and studies of it are unnecessary. I have a great deal of sympathy with that view. Nevertheless the *Quair* has a context and a meaning within Gibbon's life. He left the district in Scotland where it is set when he was little more than a boy, he forged a very personal view of human life and history, and he wrote fourteen other books. It seemed to me that a study of his development, both within the region of his birth and away from it, might reveal the forces which shaped his mind and his great book. Many people have an image of *A Scots Quair*, and perhaps of its author, without being aware of the long process of search and discovery that lay behind it.

This is not a definitive biography, and it is questionable whether the materials for one exist. There are long periods of Mitchell's life in which we cannot say with any certainty exactly where he was or what he was doing, and only the general outline is known. For a twentieth-century writer this is unusual, and from the point of view of con-structing a biographical narrative, it is unsatisfactory. We know far more about some nineteenth-century writers than we do about Leslie Mitchell. Scott or Byron, Ruskin or George Eliot lived much of their lives in public, and they created throughout their lives a continuous biographical record. Mitchell's life, until perhaps the final two years, was essentially a private life, and, like the lives of most men, it passed without record. Indeed on one level his life might be seen as a mystery story. Why was his childhood development so different from that of the children who grew up with him? How did he preserve his own unique vision of the land of his childhood through fifteen years of exile, and then re-create it in the space of a few months? As a writer, having written so many forgettable books, how did he compose an overwhelmingly original masterpiece? Why did he fail to recognise his own genius and direct it into its true channels? Why did he organise his life so irrationally, and why did he have to die? I have tried to focus on these questions, and, if it has not been possible to answer them directly, to reveal certain patterns of his inner life which throw some light on his enigmatic career.

Most of the uncertainties about Mitchell's outer life relate to the years 1919 to 1925, the period in Glasgow, in the army, and up to his marriage. It is possible that significant events did occur in these years, of which we know nothing and which further research might uncover. A number of his personal letters from this period, addressed to his future wife Rebecca, are restricted from public access until the year 2000. At the time this book was being researched, the Ministry of Defence archives containing his military records were unfortunately closed for an extended period. The one person who shared his life, his wife, died in 1978 without leaving her account of him. Ian Munro's biography, published in 1966, is immensely valuable because it was written with Rebecca's co-operation; but it clearly leaves many things unexplained, either because Rebecca did not know the answers, or because they seemed unimportant, or because she chose to keep them private. Leslie Mitchell was a man who had few intimate friends, he did not keep diaries, and wrote few very personal letters to anyone other than Rebecca. When he became a professional author, he wrote at such pressure that everything was written for publication. He revealed himself most in his books, and I have used his writings extensively as biographical evidence. This approach can easily be criticised, for one needs a sixth sense to distinguish fact from fiction. I have referred incidents in his books to his own life mainly where there is some corroborative evidence to support them. But I have referred to other cases where a fictional incident seems to bear the unmistakable imprint of personal experience, and an autobiographical basis can be assumed. Using this approach I have tried to record the outward events of his life as far as they are known, but also to interpret the development of his inner life.

What has proved virtually impossible to recapture is his personal presence: what was he really like as a man? Was he enthusiastic or cynical, dynamic or cold, selfish or generous, loud or withdrawn? Was he all these things at different times? Was he the same personality when he was a thirty-year-old professional writer as when he was a soldier of twenty? I do not know. But these things were aspects of the private man, and they vanished when he died. Our interest is not really in the private man, but in the pattern of his life and mind, which he made public in his works, and which will endure permanently.

Several people have provided invaluable help in the preparation of this book. The evocative photographs of the Mearns were taken by Richard Siwek and Stuart Rae. Isabella Williamson of the Grassic Gibbon Centre in Arbuthnott directed me to some basic sources. Douglas Young read and commented on the text, and to his book *Beyond the Sunset* I am indebted for many aspects of the interpretation of Mitchell's works. I was guided on several important points of Scottish literature and social history by Vicky Stephenson. Leslie Mitchell's two children, Daryll Mitchell and Rhea Martin, answered many questions and offered many personal insights about their parents' lives. Rhea Martin generously gave permission to quote from Mitchell's papers and to reproduce the photograph of her mother for the first time. I am most grateful to her. This book inevitably leaves many questions unanswered, but without the help of these people, it would be still more imperfect than it is.

I disapprove of dedications in books, but if this book were to be inscribed with anyone's name it would be Rebecca Middleton's. Her personality is elusive now, but without her I seriously believe that Leslie Mitchell would not have become the writer he was, and that *A Scots Quair* would have remained unwritten. Leslie Mitchell has his memorials, most importantly his creative work, and therefore this book is offered as small memorial to the woman who inspired the best of that work.

Lewis Grassic Gibbon

Chapter 1 Childhood:
The Growth of Imagination

If you travel north out of Inverbervie then take the road to the left, just before the long ascent to Kinneff begins, you enter the valley of Bervie Water. On each side the hills climb smoothly away from you, while in the distance to the west the higher Grampian mountains are clearly visible. In contrast to the main coastal highway, this road gives a distinct sense of seclusion, silence and remoteness. This sense is even stronger in the crescent-shaped combe which curves down from that road to Arbuthnott church. The deep, narrow lane, its sides wooded or walled, leads down to the deserted meads fringing Bervie water, its brooding quiet almost something from another age. There are high roads leading out of the valley to north and south, over Reisk and Garvock: their long perspectives draw the eye irresistibly up into the wide, unobstructed air.

This enclosed valley was the world in which James Leslie Mitchell spent the formative years of his childhood and youth. This was not a landscape of great beauty, except when the light or the clouds made it beautiful. It has always been a worked and working landscape. Its life was farming, the unmechanised crofts worked by the labour of each family. It was a harsh, grinding life, only one stage above bare subsistence. It was a community of few, strong traditions: its horizons and values were well-defined, and from its people it demanded conformity. This valley was the setting for the young writer's outer life. It provided the bricks from which his days and his selfhood were built – the roads he walked, the hills and woods he explored, the language he spoke. In one sense these things penetrated deep into his being. But they produced too another and equally powerful impulse in his life: the desire to escape. He fulfilled this desire by developing an inner life, in which his mind was free to range through time and space, escaping from the enclosed valley. Literature and imagination claimed him and led him into paths infinitely removed from his roots, and then paradoxically led him back to describe and interpret his first

9

"And in the east against the cobalt blue of the sky lay the shimmer of the North Sea, that was by Bervie."

world. The pattern of his life was to be one of exile and homecoming.

This valley was not his birthplace. The first six years of his life were spent further north in Aberdeenshire, on the croft of Hillhead of Seggat in the parish of Auchterless, close to the upper waters of the River Ythan. Around the large farmsteads of Seggat and Sillerton were clustered numerous small crofts (Backhill of Seggat, Bogs of Seggat, Croft of Sillerton etc.), while at the nearby Chapel of Seggat lay the ruins of a pre-Reformation church. Hillhead was a typical croft consisting of just three fields, and it was one of many farms and crofts owned by Robert Gordon's College in Aberdeen. The annual rent at £36.5.0 was high for a property of some sixty acres. The house (now sadly derelict) was a good size: two-storied with roof windows and an enclosed porch. It was naturally without electricity and its water was drawn from an outside pump. Looking out on three sides across low, sweeping hills, the site is a lonely one.

Born on 13 February 1901, Leslie Mitchell was the youngest of the three sons of James McIntosh Mitchell and Lilias Grant Gibbon. His father was a stern, unemotional man, almost forty years old when Leslie was born. His mother was just twenty-eight, warmer and more sympathetic perhaps, but the lives of both parents were rigidly fixed on the work of the farm, and as the years went by they had less and less understanding for their strangely gifted child. It seems certain that the portrait of John Guthrie in *Sunset Song* owes something to the writer's father, with the important difference that there is nowhere any suggestion that physical brutality was ever a part of James Mitchell's character. There was a warmer, more intuitive bond with his mother: when he created a new identity for himself as a Scots writer, it was her name that he chose. Yet she clearly felt compelled to suppress her feelings and to assert the more rigorous values of the crofting family: in the crises of his youth, she shared his father's expectations and disappointments, and to the end of his life there was a wounding tension with both his parents. And the Mitchell family was indeed a complex and intriguing one, for Leslie's two brothers were in fact half-brothers. Their mother, Lilias Gibbon, was born in 1873 in Leochel Cushnie near Alford, the daughter of George Gibbon, a farm labourer and his wife Lilias Grassick. She was one of a dozen children, and as for so many poor country girls, the only work open to her was to leave home and enter domestic service. In her nineteenth year she was living at Belhelvie, near the coast, and it was there that her first child, George Donald Gibbon was born in January 1893. He was registered as illegitimate, and his father was not named. Where Lilias and her child lived for the next four years is unknown, but by November 1897 she was back in Leochel Cushnie, where her second son, John Grassick Hall Gibbon, was born. He too was illegitimate, but in January 1898 Lilias entered a paternity suit naming as the father Alexander Hall, a farm servant in Banchory. It was just ten months later, on New Year's Eve 1898 in Aberdeen, that she married James Mitchell, the author's father. She was then twenty-five years old with two children by different fathers. We can only speculate on the feelings and tensions that may have existed within such a family. In fact, illegitimacy was very common in parts of rural Scotland in the nineteenth century, especially in Aberdeenshire. It was not unusual for young couples to live together for some years and start a family without actually marrying, although they often married later, after the birth of one or two children. This is surprising and puzzling to us, for it contradicts the accepted picture of a rigid, church-dominated code of behaviour; yet a study of family records demonstrates beyond doubt that it was widespread. Nor was it uncommon for a man to marry a woman who already had a child: James Mitchell himself was illegitimate, and his mother, Isabella Mitchell, had married his stepfather, the crofter William Henderson, when he was five years old.

So Leslie Mitchell was his father's only son, and yet the tension between them was always present and was always far greater than any such feeling between George and John and their stepfather. Was this because James Mitchell expected so much more from him, and was hurt and baffled by his son's unusual character, and his indifference to the farm? James Mitchell had clearly married Lily Gibbon with open eyes; but did he nevertheless feel sexual jealousy towards her? Did the descriptions of the sexual tensions within the Guthrie family in *Sunset Song* have a basis in the Mitchell family? We can only guess about this, just as we can only speculate whether Leslie Mitchell himself knew the truth about his family. Illegitimacy certainly figures in his works: the farmer who fathers children on his housekeeper, and the man who marries a woman with an illegitimate child, but who continually reproaches her for it, both appear in *Cloud Howe*. The short story 'Smeddum' turns on the secret of non-marriage. Whatever the truth may be, and it is probably now beyond recovery, it seems clear that the author's mother and father may have been more complex personalities than has been realised.

We have almost no direct biographical knowledge of Leslie's early years, but it is not difficult to trace some important features of his youth from the fictional accounts of a crofting childhood which he wrote much later, especially in his novel *The Thirteenth Disciple*, and from many other scattered references. His outline autobiography records a childhood memory which held a special significance for him: at the age of five he constructed a toy farm-wagon and yoked the family cat to it. This symbolised to him the agricultural impulse, the human urge to manipulate and dominate nature. The district around Seggat was rich in antiquities: tumuli, stone circles and cists had yielded well-documented finds of human remains, urns and bronze weapons. One mile away lay the ruins of Towie Barclay castle, and a little further was the site known as the "Bloody Butts of Lendrum", where a battle was fought in the eleventh century between the Thane of Buchan and Donald of the Isles, and where a number of ancient weapons had been found. It seems that Leslie Mitchell was keenly aware of this first world, and that his imagination was already active, for twenty years later his memory returned to his first home when constructing the geography of his novels. In *The Thirteenth Disciple* the child is born into a croft named Chapel O'Seddel, Seggat itself re-appears as Segget in *Cloud Howe* while a mile south of Seggat lay the farm of Meiklebogs.

Leslie Mitchell attended school very briefly at Auchterless, but in the year 1907 James Mitchell and his family left Hillhead of Seggat and lived for one year in the city of Aberdeen. Where they lived, and whether the children were schooled in the city, has not been discovered. The reasons for their leaving Seggat are unknown, unless the fictional account of John Guthrie's virtual expulsion from his croft was based on fact. But crofting was clearly in James Mitchell's blood, for in the spring of 1908 he had taken a lease on the croft of Bloomfield, two miles above Arbuthnott. These events are slightly telescoped in *Sunset Song* and an imaginary winter journey over the Slug Road to the new croft is memorably described early in the novel. The Guthries' fictional story begins in Echt, not such a great distance from the Mearns, yet the writer describes the new home as "far in the south": he made this tiny yet revealing slip because he was thinking of the much longer journey from Auchterless.

Bloomfield was a larger croft than Hillhead of Seggat, around seventy acres. It stands now open and exposed on all sides, but in 1909 it was bounded on the north and west by the large woodland of the Reisk plantation, felled during World War One. The site is a lonely one, but at night the lights appear in the houses and farms on the surrounding hills, and the landscape takes on an unexpected beauty, an almost visionary quality, which Leslie Mitchell often described. As farm land, Bloomfield was apparently poor and unrewarding, so that the family's life and character became increasingly harsh and demanding. The annual rent of £15.3.9. was much cheaper than Seggat. Like most of the land in the parish, Bloomfield

"Hidden away amid their yews were kirk and manse".

was part of the Arbuthnott Estate. One of the oldest estates in
Scotland, the Arbuthnott house and lands were in a ruinous state in
the years 1900-1920. Neglected for several generations, the estate was
now mortgaged, held in trust, and the home of a solitary, reclusive
earl. It was no secret that his disreputable butler controlled the house
and the home farm: this story is retold in *Sunset Song*. Leslie Mitchell
later described a fictional valley on the east of the Grampians as
"Neither Lowland nor Highland....a place without history". This
expresses so well the elusive role of the North-East within Scottish
history: the colourful, dramatic scenes that passed into Scottish
legend were played out elsewhere, in Edinburgh, Stirling, St.
Andrews, Atholl or Skye. The dimension of Scottish culture that lived
so vitally in the North-East was not affairs of kings and queens, of
feuds and governments, but the continuity of the people, the farmers
and the fishermen, whose lives reached back to a deeper sense of
Scotland than the costume-drama of Stewart history. This was a
perception which Leslie Mitchell would express again and again.

What was the reality of crofting at this time and in this region? Crofting had not the technical meaning it carried in the Western Highlands in the nineteenth century, where conditions were so poor that they could scarcely sustain even subsistence farming. In the North-East, the soil was more fertile, the leases were better, and the crofts were larger. The croft was a small farm – anything from twenty to nearly one hundred acres – worked by the farmer with family labour. It might be held on a medium-term lease from the landowner, nineteen years being the commonest term, or it might be renewed simply year by year. At the end of the lease the tenancy might be renewed, or the owner might have other plans for the croft, and the family would have to move. The highest priority was to grow the family's subsistence food crops, oats and vegetables, but additional cash crops for sale on the open market were essential too, to pay the rent, clothe the family and maintain the farm. When John Guthrie saw that "he'd be squeezed to death and he'd stand no chance" against larger farms, he was clearly thinking of profit, not of bare subsistence; and the sum of three hundred pounds which he left on his death offered his daughter a crisis of choice in her life. In this region the crofter was in competition with the large capitalist farmer whose ambitions were far higher than mere subsistence. The land was of course ploughed by horses, and the horseman's skill and pride became one of the strongest traditions of farming in this era. The crofting system created a degree of social mobility: a hard-working labourer in the North-East could always aspire to leasing a croft of his own and becoming his own master, in contrast to Southern Scotland – Lothian, Fife, the Borders – where farms were larger and the divisions between farmer and labourer were fixed for life. In a social sense the crofter cut across simple class divisions of rich or poor, in terms of his control over his own life, his independence.

But this independence was bought at the price of a harsh discipline, a remorseless creed of toil to which the entire family was subjected. We have consciously to remind ourselves of the harsh simplicity, verging on personal deprivation, of such a rural childhood at the turn of the century. For the children of poor families, the fabric of life was stark and simple: personal possessions, toys, books, entertainments, sports, holidays, travel, all these were almost non-existent. The games

they played, the culture which children will always create, these were
their own, shaped from the elementary materials of their environment. Even more important than the outward simplicity of their lives,
was the balance of relationships within the family. Children were
expected to conform absolutely to standards set by their parents: the
child had to fit in to the parents' world. There was no concept of a
child-centred relationship. It was expected that the child would follow
its parents in the occupation of crofting. Virtually every child at
Arbuthnott village school would be destined for farm work or
domestic service. The vast majority of children would leave school at
fourteen and begin to contribute to the household economy. The
Education Act of 1872 was extremely important in releasing young
children from some of the rigours of farm work, requiring them to
attend village schools, usually between the ages of six and fourteen.
Before the 1872 Act many crofting children would not have attended
school at all, but have helped around the farm from the age of six
onwards. In that sense, the education reforms of the late nineteenth
century certainly played a part in undermining the crofting tradition.
The emotional relationships within this working family were normally
quite distant and undemonstrative, the father in particular remaining
a stern, remote figure. He directed the work of the farm, which was
the basis of the family's life, and all other relationships were
secondary to that overwhelming fact. It is not too radical to say that
these children really had no childhood, in the sense that we would
recognise it today. After the first years of infancy, they were seen as
miniature adults. This is not to suggest that the children were cruelly
treated, but that within the values and traditions of that society,
children were allowed a strictly limited role, subservient to the
economic demands of the parents. There was no expectation that a
child would display unusual talents, adopt an unusual career, or seek
self-fulfilment outside the community where it grew up. The growth of
the child's personality, a child's right to develop in its own way, the
shaping of an emotional relationship through warmth, understanding
and play, all these concepts were quite foreign to the society in which
Leslie Mitchell grew up. This is crucial to an understanding of
Mitchell's childhood. Somehow he was determined to carve out for
himself a space, an identity that transcended these conventions. The

conflicts of his early life sprang from this single-minded quest, which was nothing less than the quest for his own selfhood. One of his most striking qualities, unmistakable even in the records of his childhood, was his independence, his determination to shape his own life, a self-awareness which could easily appear to others to be arrogance.

Leslie Mitchell's quest for a wider world beyond the farms of the Mearns was, in one sense, part of a historical process. The decline in crofting in the Grampians between 1870 and 1930 – during the lifetime of his father – was remorseless: each year the total number of agricultural holdings was falling, the number of small holdings (i.e. below fifty acres) was falling, and the number of holdings in proportion to the population was falling. The sources of this decline were twofold: the competition from the larger farms, and the impact of cultural changes such as education and mobility. At the beginning of this period, during a few crucial years from 1865 to 1880, the value of food imports into Britain doubled, as grains and refrigerated meat poured in from North and South America and from the Empire, creating a crisis in British agriculture. Crofting had flourished in the Grampians in the nineteenth century when there was a large rural population and no other form of employment. It suffered with the historic fall in prices, and with improved access to education and information. Migration to the great cities of Scotland, and beyond to the farms of Canada or Australia or Argentina, seemed to offer a chance of a better life than the traditional croft. Emigration and the movement of people from the land became an everyday fact in these communities. At the age of twelve, Leslie Mitchell would write in a school essay "The barrenness of the country had made emigration common in Scotland ... Often people make their fortunes in a few years, when at home it would be a great difficulty to make one in a lifetime". And yet the crofters' independence, their partial freedom from the market permitted them to cling stubbornly to their traditions. Perhaps the decline in crofting is less remarkable than its vigour: as late as 1939 the total number of agricultural holdings in the modern Grampian region was 16,000, of which over a half were still below fifty acres.

Perhaps once in a generation, a child born into such an enclosed world is destined from an early age to see beyond its confines, and not merely to rebel intuitively against its values but to articulate that rebellion. Why a certain child should be gifted with this faculty, while his friends and brothers who completely shared his world were not, will always remain a mystery. At the age of ten, Leslie Mitchell was already the odd one out at school, remembered by his contemporaries as perpetually absorbed in books while they were playing, and by his two older brothers, George and John, as unwilling to spare time from his reading to help with the farm chores. John later recalled:

> I can mind when we were boys he was the quiet one, always wanting to be on his own. After school the rest of us would play about, while he made straight home to read whatever he could lay his hands on. There wasn't much in those days, but he made do with what there was, anything at all, newspapers, magazines, The People's Friend, even the backs of cigarette cards. He could never get enough to satisfy his appetite for books, and his thirst for information. There was no doubt he knew what he wanted. Whiles mother would say 'Leslie, would you like to get some wood for the fire'. He'd look up from his book and say quietly 'No mother'. And often he'd get away with it. One of us would have to do the job and he'd go on with his reading. And he remembered everything he read or heard. He had a wonderful memory.

The importance of the village school as a stimulus in the lives of these children can hardly be exaggerated, although its course of study now seems stark enough. Leslie Mitchell set down his memory of it in one of his novels:

> There was practically no religious teaching. History was circumscribed enough, but the dates were enlivened with figures like Malcolm Canmore and Mary Queen of Scots, whose blood was lapped by a dog. Arithmetic was taught on a straightforward plan, geography was no dull subject, and being Scots, they found English fascinating enough. They were told to open their mouths, to roll the letter 'r' and to avoid the elision of aitches, otherwise they might be mistaken for Englishmen – poor, cowardly, excitable people, whom Scotsmen had chased across the border again and again... Science did not exist... Drawing was a smudging of paper with unrecognisable objects... No music was taught.

The childish sense of kinships and enmities, of a hierarchy based on small signs and qualifications, has always been developed at elementary school, as Mitchell noticed:

> Most of the pupils came from some distance and brought sandwiches for

"Hurrying through the park paths till she came out above kirkyard and manse".

lunch... One's social status was graded according to the contents of one's food-parcel. Poor children, and the children of ploughmen, brought pieces of bread and jam, and were consequently pariahs; sons of small farmers like the Maudslays of Chappel O'Seddel, brought oatcakes and butter and home-made cheese and soda-scones...the children of the factor, the postmaster and forester unrolled ham sandwiches, buns and cream biscuits.

Two people who were to influence his future now came into his life: his schoolmaster and his future wife. In 1913 Alexander Gray, a sympathetic young graduate of Aberdeen University arrived in Arbuthnott as village schoolmaster. He recognised Mitchell's unusual gifts, lent him books, treasured his schoolboy essays, the only ones he ever kept, and provided him with an intellectual friendship which lasted throughout his life. Each day Mitchell and his brothers trekked almost three miles from Bloomfield to the village school – he later calculated that he had walked 14,000 miles in the quest of education.

It is scarcely surprising that there are no photographs of the

Mitchell family in these early years, or of Leslie as a child, other than
a glimpse in a Sunday-school group photograph. We have little idea of
his physical appearance, although Alexander Gray remembered him
as a slightly awkward boy, walking with a stoop, looking down as if
lost in thought. Gray thought him:

> Sensitive, lonely, introspective... He was the only boy I ever saw hoeing
> turnips with an open book in his hand... Not bothering much with the
> other boys' games and adventures, but always friendly and kind,
> especially to the younger ones... I asked him once 'Where do you get your
> brains from Leslie?' He replied shyly but proudly 'From my mother'.

The library of the minister, Peter Dunn, was also thrown open to
the young scholar. Both Mitchell's parents were described by those
who knew them as God-fearing Presbyterians, although it was also
recalled that while his mother attended church with the children, his
father did not. The church, one of the oldest parish churches in
Scotland, became very familiar to Leslie: with its fifteenth century
Allardice memorial and its Victorian stained-glass window, it became
one of the starting-points of *Sunset Song*. Among the names on the
gravestones in the churchyard he must have seen that of Tavendale.
In 1928 Peter Dunn left for America, where he took charge of a
Scottish church in Boston, an event which left its mark on the career
of the Reverend Gibbon in *Sunset Song*.

It was recalled by Alexander Gray and others that from an early
age Leslie Mitchell took pains to speak in cool, standard English, the
language that was necessary then if a country child wished to get on in
the wider world. In the conflict between English and Scots language
and culture, English represented to the young Mitchell escape into the
wider world beyond the Mearns. It is an intriguing but unanswered
question whether he was aware of Scots vernacular literature, such as
J. M. Barrie, Douglas Brown, or William Alexander. If he was, he
reacted against that tradition: at this early stage in his life, literature
was universal not local, its power was precisely that it revealed worlds
that lay beyond North-East Scotland. The perception that aspects of
ultimate reality might be revealed through a sense of place, through
the people and the language of rural Scotland, lay in the future.

More important still than Alexander Gray, on the neighbouring
croft of Hareden lived the Middleton family, whose daughter

Rebecca, was to become Mitchell's wife, although they were not childhood sweethearts. Rebecca later wrote:

> I remember it so clearly, a beautiful sunny morning, the first time I saw Leslie Mitchell... He was a strange, unusual boy, and looked so very distant. I disliked him at first sight. I liked his brothers George and John much better. I certainly never dreamed Leslie would one day marry me. As I saw more of Leslie Mitchell, I realised that he was different. Quiet and withdrawn, seldom playing like a boy, engrossed in his book, reading whenever he got the chance – and when his father would let him. Mr Mitchell had little time for books and he let his son know it.

During the coming years, Rebecca and Leslie would often walk to school together, and they grew gradually closer. Rebecca's father Robert was easily recognised by those who knew him as the model for Long Rob of the Mill in *Sunset Song*, famous locally for his stories of horses and his agnosticism. Mitchell may have felt more at ease in such company at Hareden than he did at Bloomfield, for already his inner development was alienating him from his family. He had conceived a passion for the past, and spent hours exploring the fields and moors searching for tools and weapons of flint or iron left by ancient dwellers of the Mearns. Within a two-mile radius of Bloomfield there were standing stones, stone cists, and the site of a prehistoric camp, as well as more recent historic remains – an ancient chapel, fragments of a castle, and a saint's well. The Standing Stone on Murrystone Hill and the cairns of Montgoldrum were within sight of Bloomfield. This enthusiasm was to remain one of the most enduring strands in his thought throughout his life. He developed an intimate sense of the locality, the tracks, the rivers, the farms, the woods that had been settled and worked by generations of forgotten people. He later coined the expressive phrase "the ancient library of the hills" to describe his feeling for these long-dead people and the landscape they inhabited. And for all his bookishness, for all his distaste for the mire and labour of the croft, his observation was keen and his memory was sharp: the life of the farm and the details of the landscape were richly and accurately recaptured when he wrote of them twenty years later.

He was fascinated too by astronomy, by the immensity of the night sky, and he taught himself to recognise the stars, planets and constellations. A fictional account of his star-watching in one of his novels has the unmistakable ring of truth: he had borrowed a telescope from the minister, and had induced his father to look through it at the heavens. His father's reaction was:

> 'Aye. Aye. But what's the use o' it laddie? Y'll no get on in the world through lookin' at stars. Come awa in.' From that moment Malcom hated him – single-mindedly, ruthlessly, as only an intelligent child can hate.

He read books that fed his enthusiasms for history and science, both serious works (including, reportedly, *The Origin of Species* when he was thirteen) and adventure stories that stretched his imagination – Rider Haggard, Conan Doyle, H. G. Wells – writers whose fantasies explored worlds distant in space and time. His parents could not see where his imagination was leading him: the only non-farming careers they knew were minister or schoolmaster, and Mitchell showed no interest in either. There is no record that he was attempting to write at this early age: aside from his school essays and private letters nothing that he wrote before 1921 has survived. Normally Leslie would have left school at the age of fourteen, in 1915, but his talents were recognised and despite his parents' reluctance, he was placed in a "feeder" class where outstanding pupils were prepared with an additional academic year to try for a place at a high school, in this case Mackie Academy, Stonehaven. Years later when writing of the farm childhood of Mungo Park, Mitchell projected onto the young explorer his own distaste for the mire of the farm and the dourness of the people. He clearly identified learning and literature as an escape route from this world, and in his description of Park he gave a glimpse of his own personality at this time: "He invented the proper resistance: gravity of outward demeanour to hide the burgeon of his soul beneath".

Alexander Gray showed remarkable foresight in preserving Mitchell's school essay books from the years 1913 to 1915. Some of them appear to have been set subjects, but most must have been selected by Leslie Mitchell himself. Some of them appear to have been written in the classroom, since they occasionally end virtually in mid-flow, without concluding the argument, while others are longer and more finished, suggesting that they were composed at home. The titles alone give an immediate insight into his mind at this time:

"In the lower half of the tower was an effigy-thing of Cospatric de Gondeshil, him that killed the Gryphon."

Emigration, Bucaneers, The Discovery of America, Invaders of Britain, The Romans in Caledonia, The Destruction of Pompeii, The Decay of Cities. Some of these are formal essays written to demonstrate the child's knowledge, some are dramatic reconstructions of history, while others are reflective and descriptive. The themes of travel, discovery, and historical drama are dominant. Very few are concerned with the people or the places he knew personally: his imagination inhabited the world beyond the Mearns. In an essay entitled "A Continental Tour: The Balkans 1912" he wrote:

> As I was now the heir to a large fortune (£60,000) I resolved to tour through the Balkans. As the Bulgarians had not yet advanced I visited the famous city of Hadrian. But it would take too long to tell of how I saw pitched battles, walked along the Golden Horn, strolled through the onetime capital of the world, rowed across the mighty Danube, climbed the Pindus or visited the isles of the Blest.

Essays like these display an extremely wide range of historical reference, evidence of his obsessive reading and retentive memory. Many of these pieces are exceptionally well written, showing a mastery of long, complex sentences and an ability to shape ideas. It is clear that he deliberately cultivated a literary style modelled on his favourite authors – Scott, Lytton and Ballantyne. By contrast, in his description of "A Snowstorm", there appears a brief sentence that is perfect in its simplicity and clarity: "The storm did not abate that night, the windows shook and the wind whistled, making sleep impossible". Throughout these essays we recognise motifs that would appear in his mature masterpiece, and which were clearly already part of the fabric of his experience. Describing a spring morning he writes of "The wailing cry of the lapwings" newly returned after the winter, while another essay is entitled "Seed Time". It is clear that his imagination inhabited a world that was purely literary and historical: he apparently had no experience of visual art, and both here and in his mature works there is scarcely a single reference to music.

There are hints in these essays of the conflicts which his personal, intellectual development would cause, as he moved from childhood to adolescence. By the age of thirteen he was already disillusioned with religion, and he was aware of the stirrings of political consciousness. In an essay on Christmas, he described Christian history as "The long years of havoc and torture and horrible cruelty", and reflects that "Today and for the last twenty years it is an undeniable fact that the Christian religion is declining. But 'tis not before the Indian Boodh, the Chinese Confucius, or the Arab Mohamed, but before that cold, cool demon with its undefeatable energy and heavy entrenched facts – Science." In the early months of World War One, he wrote on what sounds very much like a set subject "War, Its Good and Evil":

> Oliver Cromwell wiped out one of the greatest curses of Britain, the absolute monarchy, even as the allies are to wipe out the greatest curse of Europe – Prussian militarism. But the evils of war are the horrible atrocities, the anxiety, the horrible lust for blood that gathers even in the heart of the civilised soldier.

It seems probable that the war was a decisive factor in the young Mitchell's growing alienation from his environment. After the initial fervour for the war, which he himself shared, had cooled, he saw beyond the patriotism to the cruel reality which most people on the home front chose to ignore. As early as January 1915 he wrote:

> The difference between this war and any other that was ever waged cannot be realised by some people in Arbuthnott. Today is the 56th birthday of His Imperial Majesty, the Kaiser of Germany, Belgium and Poland etc., Admiral of the Atlantic, Prince of Butchers. By this time nearly everyone in Arbuthnott imagined that our 'Kilties' would be dancing the 'Highland Fling' on the battlements of Berlin. Alas and alack for our hope! I do really think some few of us are getting down-hearted.

The surviving essay books come to a tantalising end early in 1915, just when it seems that Mitchell was beginning to develop a number of original ideas concerning his own life and that of his community. A fully articulated guide to his state of mind as he grew into young manhood is found in the dramatised accounts of the characters in his early fictions *Stained Radiance* and *The Thirteenth Disciple*. Of course, these were written a dozen years later or more, with the perspective that time brings. Yet in the unpublished outline of his autobiography, Mitchell names these books explicitly as pictures of his early life, and we are justified in treating them as accurate reflections of his inner life. The principal characters in these books were born and raised in crofting families in Aberdeenshire, and recall their childhoods in terms of bitter regret: "A grey, grey life, dull and grey in its routine, a beastly life..."; "Tears were in Thea's eyes, bitter tears, tears of an overmastering, heart-breaking pity. She and her parents were poles apart in all sympathies... In her youth they had loved her, thwarted her, misunderstood her. She had hated them...". It is clear from these passages and from the later course of his relationship with his parents that he suffered a deep sense of alienation from his family and their world. He saw their lives as a narrow meaningless enslavement to the farm work, which shrivelled both their minds and their hearts. His own intuitive understanding, his intellectual curiosity, and above all his aching, inarticulate love were unanswered:

> He never loved his mother except at odd moments when she came to his aid in matters of milk and unbuttoning, when he was very young and overcome with weariness and her hands were kind. But such occasions were few enough. Her hands were too roughened and too busy to be kind for long. Behind that immemorial gravity of hers, it was difficult to know how she looked on her children: but hardly at all as intimately *her*

children, he came to think, she had no passionate loves and no passionate dislikes.

But he reacted not simply with a personal enmity to his family, but with a deepening social anger. He sensed that it was society itself which had destroyed their human warmth and their freedom. How this had happened he did not yet know, but the pattern of economic slavery and consequent human degradation was all too clear to him. He seems never to have doubted that this was essentially a historical process, never to have accepted the religious premise that the evil lay in men's hearts. In his exploration of the landscape of the Mearns, perhaps the deepest impression was left on him by the ruins of Dunnottar Castle, with its brooding memories of the cruelties of history. This fed in him a growing anger against society's ruling powers, who he believed still degraded the lives of the common people, but with subtler means now than in the seventeenth century. He later encapsulated his sense of alienation in the phrase "the walls of the world", which conveys the loneliness and weakness of the individual confronted by a hostile society. Is it fanciful to see in this phrase the image of the stone walls of the castles, churches and mansions, whose masters had, he believed, excluded and impoverished the common people throughout history?

Thus his conflict with his family and his community existed on an emotional and an intellectual level. The paradox which he could not resolve was that they willingly embraced the harsh, ceaseless farm labour and their reward, he considered, was to be robbed of their emotional life, of freedom and of dignity. He saw his community as founded upon the same creed of servitude and repression, and it baffled him that others did not see what he saw. The dominant intellectual power in this community – the kirk – also now aroused his hostility. He regarded religion in Scotland as being emptied of all feeling for the divine and the mysterious, and being hardened into a mere code of laws. To him religion came to be associated with the process of historical corruption of human innocence. Reading works such as Foxe's *Book of Martyrs* rather than inspiring him with fervent religious feeling, filled him with loathing and caused nightmares.

This picture of his inner development is as far removed as it could possibly be from a pastoral idyll, an innocent childhood in the beauty

"High up, crowning the rock, were the ruins of the castle walls."

of the Mearns landscape. That image exists only in the modern imagination, almost a century after Leslie Mitchell was growing up. It is clear from all his writings that this landscape and man's relation to it did indeed become vital and permanent elements of his imagination. But the reality behind the landscape, the lives of the people who inhabited it, these were what mattered to him. His bleak crofting childhood and his impassioned reading of history fused in his mind and destroyed any false ideals: this paradise had too many shadows. He was a mirror of his community, but the mirror was darkened. He saw and felt too deeply, and he paid the price. The war and the general reaction to it served to focus all his sense of alienation. He felt increasingly ill at ease, and his established method of escape into literature, would, perhaps inevitably, be followed by self-exile from the place where he had grown so painfully into maturity. The strengths of this community, the courage and vitality of its people, their dignity and independence, he could not yet see nor understand. Certain parallels between Lewis Grassic Gibbon and D. H. Lawrence and James Joyce will be suggested several times during this book. Already it will be clear that their painful discovery of their own selfhood against a hostile social background, and the emotional tensions within their families, form the first link between them. Joyce's feelings for Ireland might have been Mitchell's for his community: "The soul...has a slow and dark birth, more mysterious than the birth of the body. When the soul of a man is born in this country there are nets flung at it to hold it back from flight. You talk to me of nationality, language, religion. I shall try to fly by those nets."

Mitchell's adolescent crisis deepened when, having won a place at Mackie Academy, Stonehaven in 1916, he failed to settle there. Although clearly brilliant in some ways – one of his essays was read out before the whole school – he cared only for the study of literature and history, he appeared arrogant and rebellious to his new teachers, and he made no friends. He acquired the eloquent nickname of Caliban, and was clearly branded an outsider. Rebecca Middleton was also at the school, but there is no record of how close their relationship was at this time, and her presence was clearly unable to reconcile him to his new environment. The dry, analytical approach to the literature for which he had such a strong feeling, repelled him. Alexander Gray (himself a former pupil of Mackie Academy) was called upon to mediate in a number of conflicts. But Mitchell ran away from home and attempted to join the army. Finally after a confrontation with a teacher, he stormed out of the school, never to return. His account of the incident in *The Thirteenth Disciple* centres on his teacher's accusation that he was a socialist and therefore pro-German, to which he reacted with anger and contempt. If the first of these charges was true, it confirms that the sixteen-year-old schoolboy was already consciously forging his own political and intellectual creed. The war was to figure as a powerful force in some of his later writing, and this is further confirmation of its personal impact on him at the time. Had he stayed at the school, and progressed to university, the course of his life would have been radically different. But this was one of a number of occasions when his pride became wilfulness, when the assertion of his independence became all-important, and there was undoubtedly an element of irrationality in his nature.

This public disgrace at the school created bitter dissension within his family, destroying, as they saw it, his claims to scholarly privileges. His quest for selfhood had led him into rebellion and loneliness, and had now become a self-fulfilling prophecy: already an exile in spirit, he had no choice but to become literally an exile from this world of the Mearns. His childhood, the first phase of his life, was ended. Resisting his family's pressure to take a fee as farm worker, at the age of seventeen he found himself a job as junior reporter with the Aberdeen Journal. He left home, to return in future only as visitor and, increasingly, as a stranger. Mitchell might have echoed James Joyce's famous youthful manifesto, published in 1916: "I will tell you what I will do and what I will not do. I will not serve that in which I no longer believe, whether it call itself my home, my fatherland or my church; and I will try to express myself in some mode of life or art as freely as I can and as wholly as I can, using for my defence the only arms I allow myself to use, silence, exile and cunning."

But the growth of his imagination was already complete: his selfhood had crystallised in a way that he could neither alter nor understand. Why? Why did he, among all the children in the Mearns, become first a problem child and then later a writer of genius? What caused his imagination to grow in a way so unlike that of the other children? What was it deep in his inheritance or deep in his mind that was so different? This is the unanswered and perhaps unanswerable question about Leslie Mitchell's childhood. History and biography can describe, but not ultimately explain. In a sense, this enigma was his problem too: the problem of his relationship to the land and people of his birth. He would spend years of his life as a soldier, travel to distant parts of the world, and finally settle near London. While creating a successful literary career for himself, he would follow a complex path of intellectual discovery, exploring history, philosophy, social and political theory. But ultimately he would be impelled to return to his roots, to search his memory and his imagination in order to reinterpret his own life and the life of his people with a new understanding and with an entirely new language.

"Girdling Stonehaven, down to its bay, shining and white, the sun was out."

Chapter 2 Manhood:
The Walls of the World

It was in the autumn of 1917 that the young Leslie Mitchell went to live and work in Aberdeen, lodging in St. Mary's Place. As a junior reporter he was given the job of patrolling the harbour and dock area each day, picking up stories and making contacts. After the frustrations of school he welcomed the challenge of entering the adult world, and he was, in a sense, making his living as a professional writer as he had always wished to. Already he had sensed intuitively the forces which shape the lives of people and of society, and he had now become a participant in the realities of city life – work, money, new friendships and enmities, humour, poverty, suffering. The war had had a very direct impact on Aberdeen. Trawlers were attacked by German U-boats, and Zeppelins were seen in the skies. More than 5,000 men from the city and its surroundings died in the fighting, and in the summer of 1918 there was a much-publicised demonstration against the cost of the apparently unending conflict. In December, just a month after the armistice, there was much excitement in the newspapers over the discovery that a group of Bolsheviks was active in the city. This was clearly a wider, more exciting world than that of Arbuthnott or Stonehaven, a more vibrant place than the traditional grey-stone image suggests. Yet the symbolic character of Aberdeen stone impressed him as it has many others, so that his abiding memory of the city was of

> Granite, grey granite, in birth, in puberty, adolescence, grey granite encasing the bridal room, grey granite the rooms of blear-eyed old age... One detests Aberdeen with the detestation of a thwarted lover. It is the one haunting and exasperatingly lovable city in Scotland – its fascination as inescapable as its shining mail.

Among the many hints and clues to Mitchell's youthful reading and intellectual development, it is slightly surprising that we have no knowledge of precisely when or how he first encountered socialism. There is a tradition that there was a roadmender in Arbuthnott named Charlie Smith who was a socialist, that Mitchell had long arguments with him, and that he became in part the model for Chae Strachan in *Sunset Song*. Mitchell's childhood alienation from his family's way of life would certainly predispose him towards a creed of radical social change, but we have no specific account of his political awakening. He certainly read William Morris, Wells, Shaw, and others, but when? In *The Thirteenth Disciple* he would write of the pioneer socialists:

> Here were people who, like himself, had shuddered in sick horror at the sight of the dehumanised and wandering crucified; people also who had known the challenge of the winters' stars and seen the solution of all the earth's bitter cruelties in a gigantic expedition against the World's Walls.

What is certain is that by this period in Aberdeen, Mitchell was consciously a socialist, with revolutionary sympathies. He recalled his youthful idealism in later writings, the days when "we were so young and full of dreams we could not sleep o'nights"; and in a famous passage he described

> The founding of the Aberdeen Soviet when the news of the Bolshevik Revolution came through from Russia; and how I and a cub reporter from another paper attended the foundation meeting; and were elected to the Soviet Council, forgetting we were press-men.

Aberdeen had not the degree of poverty and misery that was visible in major industrial cities like Glasgow or Liverpool, but it could still provide Mitchell with scenes he would not forget, such as the old men and the unemployed sitting hopelessly in the rain on the steps of the Wallace statue: "Wallace fascinates them you would say. He belongs to a past they dare not achieve, they have come to such horrific future as he never visioned".

But for the seventeen-year-old, the adult world had other new experiences too, including inevitably falling in love. Rebecca Middleton visited him in Aberdeen and they went to the theatre together, but he was also briefly infatuated with Margaret Miller, a girl working in the offices of the *Aberdeen Journal*. He seems to have made little progress with her and was condemned to admire her from a distance. He addressed a long, effusive poem to her, which she kept for the next fifty years:

...And so I'll sing a song of Marguerite,
She who is lovely, smiling-eyed and sweet...
For in your eyes are things that do not cease:
Wistfulness, joy, and a quiet touch of peace,
Like to the shadows, that as daylight goes,
The sun casts where the silent streamlet flows...
To watch a careless tendril of your hair
Caressed across your cheek by the still air
And see your lips with just that lingering smile
Banish the dusk and dimness of the while...

Mitchell did not regard this poem as totally serious – some of it is ironic and mock-heroic. In thought and style it is entirely conventional and could have been derived from Christina Rossetti, Meredith, or even Tennyson. Yet it is obviously the work of a practising poet, and it seems certain that he was experimenting with poetry and other forms of writing at this time, although none of it has survived. He later wrote:

> I used to sit and attempt my first novel and the wind used to come in during my absence and cart pages of my masterpiece out through the window, and Mrs M. would go chasing select extracts of J. Leslie Mitchell all over St. Mary's Place.

The period in Aberdeen lasted nearly eighteen months, and they were creative and stimulating ones. His ambition to write and his independent choice of a career had so far been justified. He probably had a general plan to build a career in journalism, possibly aspiring to more literary work in Edinburgh or London, as a basis on which to develop his talents as a creative writer. But his next move, and the experiences which followed were to destroy that future.

In February 1919 Mitchell moved to Glasgow to become a reporter on the *Scottish Farmer*. He lodged in Hill Street, unaware for some time that the house was partly a brothel. His wage was £2.5.0 per week, almost double that of a young fee'd farmworker. Glasgow shocked and appalled Mitchell. Not merely its size, but the physical squalor, the scars of industrialism, the evidence of poverty and ill-health – all these had a searing effect on his mind. He always wrote of Glasgow in terms that were ferocious, almost apocalyptic, using the

"Just clouds, they passed and finished, dissolved and were done."

metaphors of disease, enslavement and corruption to evoke its urban desolation. He had never visited any city other than Aberdeen before, and in comparison with Glasgow, Aberdeen had retained its historic character as a large market-town and fishing-port. Aberdeen's population at this time was less than 150,000, while Glasgow's was five times greater and its industry, its slums, its immigrant population was on quite another scale from that of Aberdeen. It was here that Mitchell really awoke to radical politics: Glasgow gave a specific political dimension to the intuitive anger which crofting had aroused in him. The harshness of crofting might impoverish the emotional life, but in Glasgow the mechanism of a great industrial city and the inbuilt injustice of society consumed and destroyed lives by the thousand. Like many others on Clydeside at that time, he was convinced that only the most radical solutions were possible, and he joined a group of communists. Mitchell's official political allegiance and activities during the rest of his life remain an enigma. Although he described himself variously as a socialist, a communist, a

Trotskyist, or a revolutionary, there is no evidence that he ever belonged to any political party, or took part in any political campaigning, except for these few months in Glasgow. Like many other writers in the 1920s and 1930s, his weapon was his voice. He arrived in Glasgow during Red Clydeside's great days of 1919, when the government was convinced it had a Bolshevik uprising on its hands, when the red flag was brandished at demonstrations, and John Maclean was appointed by Lenin the first Soviet Consul for Scotland. Was this socialist activity perhaps part of his reason for moving to Glasgow? Exactly what Mitchell did, or which group he participated in is unknown, yet his later accounts of the workings of political groups, from his first novel *Stained Radiance* to *Grey Granite*, suggest that he was for a time closely involved in its organisation. They also indicate that he had no illusions about their methods or their morality: to the serious revolutionary, the end always justified the means.

This doctrine led him into personal disaster. In his desire to further their cause, he gave them money which he obtained by falsifying his expense claims at the *Scottish Farmer*. After only a few months when the total sum involved amounted to £60, he was discovered and dismissed. The offence was trivial, and thousands of people have done the same thing with impunity. Yet to him it was a profound disgrace: the implications it would have for his future vis-à-vis his family, coupled with the tensions which Glasgow had set up in him, overwhelmed him, and he attempted suicide by taking laudanum. He recovered after hospital treatment and returned to his family at Bloomfield. He was not ill physically, but his life was at a crisis. On a pragmatic level, any further work in journalism, in Scotland at least, would be closed to him. On a deeper level he understandably felt a sense of defeat. Neither his experiments with writing nor his political ideals had made any impression on the outside world. The walls of the world were too strong. Tension with his family now reached its worst pitch. They felt that, having pursued his own ambitions and having failed, he should now conform and return to farm life. His brother John recalled fierce arguments between Leslie and his father, in which Leslie vowed he would tramp the roads rather than take a fee. The family hostility was based on their incomprehension of their son's mind and motives. But it was pragmatic too: a grown-up son could not consume the food of the farm without working for it: the crofting family tradition was based on hard economics, not emotional support. He may have seen Rebecca Middleton at this time, but of what passed between them there is no record.

Again, as in the crisis at Mackie Academy, Mitchell's only course was to escape, and again his action had a hint of desperation and irrationality: he joined the army. It is ironic that having rebelled against the norms of his upbringing he should have taken this traditional escape route from poverty or unemployment. It is often said that he joined the army because he wished to travel. But in itself this scarcely carries conviction. At this stage he had never shown a wish to travel: he had never even visited Edinburgh or London. Nor could he know for certain that he would be sent abroad – he might have spent years in military camps in England. Since he must also have foreseen that he would hate the army, his action must have had a deeper, less rational motive: it was to swallow up his sense of failure, an act of self-abnegation. The army would feed him, take him far from home, and dissolve his previous identity. There was surely no logical reason why he could not have resumed journalism in some form, in London for example, where the months with the *Scottish Farmer* could have been easily concealed. Nor did he attempt to find other congenial work such as publishing or bookselling for example. Perhaps he lacked both the means and the will to search for such opportunities. There is every indication that he sought a complete break with his old life, even if that break were self-destructive.

On 26 August 1919 Mitchell entered the Royal Army Service Corps, and within a few months he was in the Middle East. Over the next three years he was stationed in Egypt, Palestine, Mesopotamia and Persia. After the disintegration of Turkish rule in the Middle East, the British were heavily involved in administering League of Nations mandates to bring new states into being. Mitchell was never personally in action, but he saw at first hand the violence, confusion and squalor of that region at that time. Throughout the summer of 1920 there was serious guerilla warfare with Arab tribesmen of the future Iraq, to which Mitchell was a personal witness. On one level he hated the army life. An essentially private man in thought and feeling, he would inevitably become the odd man out, and he detested the coarseness of barrackroom culture. He described the English soldier as "that most cowardly, helpless and brainless of beings". The fiercest expression of his disgust with the army is surely the transformation of Ewan Tavendale's character after enlisting, when all pride and sensitivity are replaced by brutality. Yet at the same time the army suited him somehow. To be in the land of the ancient civilisations he had read and dreamed of was in itself an immensely important experience for Mitchell. He visited the cities of Constantinople, Cairo, Jerusalem and Alexandria, saw the Pyramids, rode the deserts of the Holy Land on a camel, and saw the Christmas pilgrims at Bethlehem. On a deeper level, the army intrigued him as a revelation of humanity. He felt the need to share the anonymity and degradation of the common man, to be "among the filthy, filthy too." At the heart of the trauma of the Glasgow slums was the realisation that these were people, like himself, but poor, sick, degraded and hopeless. The feeling of oneness with the sufferings of common humanity would be repeatedly expressed in his novels, and was the driving force of Spartacus and of the mature Ewan Tavendale. Mitchell may have accepted army life almost as martyrdom, a radical distancing from his previous life. Throughout this period we have to think of his mind not as learning and growing but as passive and waiting, content simply to experience and exist. And inevitably he made friends too: shared experiences will create camaraderie among the most disparate people. Army life for Mitchell, though almost always disagreeable, was not a wasted experience. From his army colleagues he undoubtedly learned much about the reality of the war that had ended only a year earlier, and whose shadow was to fall over much of his writing.

Throughout these three years he corresponded with Rebecca Middleton, who was now living in London and working as a Civil Servant, and he saw her when on leave. It is possible that he also visited Paris while on leave, since he refers several times in his writings to Paris as if he knew the city personally. His letters to Rebecca were, forgivably, self-dramatising and romantic: "I am without a future or a care for it, disreputable, a dreamer of dreams." But it is equally clear that she was by now his trusted friend and confessor, that he could speak to her on an intellectual level as to no

"A circle of stones from olden times."

one else. Moreover their long friendship was now acknowledged to be deepening into love. In November 1921 he was writing "When you and I are married...", and in February 1922 he addressed a poem to her written "in exile" in Palestine:

> Out of the darkness, softly shod, you come
> With perfumed hair;
> Hands that are warmly trembling to the touch,
> And bosom bare.
>
> And bending low (as once of old you did)
> With slender grace,
> Like dew to thirsting desert sands, I feel
> Your kiss upon my face.
>
> And know, when comes the first still glint of dawn,
> Grey-barred and clear –
> Your soul has crossed the sundering leagues of sea
> And loved me here!

Out of these years in the Middle East would come many of the themes of his later books. In his childhood in the Mearns he had cultivated an inner life and conceived the desire to write. But to write directly from the inner life alone requires the insight of a mystic or poet of the highest order. Most writing, including most novels, emerges from the encounter with reality. For Mitchell, the period in Aberdeen and Glasgow began that process, but his experiences in the army added a further dimension.

The themes that were present in his childhood and which acquired greater weight from his Middle East travels were many: the theme of exploration as the escape from self; the theme of religion, whose creative and destructive aspects impressed him so forcibly in this region, where the three great historical religions were born; the theme of history, sharpened by the opportunity to see the monuments of ancient civilisations, monuments that were contemporary with the stone circles and cists of the Mearns, but so different in scale and character. All these intellectual forces worked in his mind against the harsh, squalid background of the Middle East and the dehumanisation of army life. This was clearly a potent mixture, and it had far-reaching consequences for his later thinking about society, history, religion and humanity. If he could come to terms with these impressions, interpret them and set them within a conceptual framework, he might perhaps make sense of his own life, and create from them mature works of literature.

He was discharged from the army on 22 March 1923, and the five months that followed are the most mysterious in Mitchell's adult life. He did not return to his family or to Scotland, but went to London. If he tried to find work as a journalist again, he did not succeed. And, most significant of all, he did not marry Rebecca Middleton. All later accounts of this period are imprecise, and we must assume that, after the deepening intimacy of 1921-22, they had quarrelled, either by letter or after Mitchell arrived in London. According to his later accounts, he attempted to live by writing and produced stories and essays for which he could find no publisher. Hardship turned to desperation and, like Malcom Maudslay in *The Thirteenth Disciple*, he was reduced briefly to becoming a door-to-door salesman. Admitting defeat, he once again escaped from failure and from the world's hostility be re-joining the services, enlisting this time in the RAF on 31 August 1923. Afterwards he wrote bitterly "We are, nearly all we soldiers, failures in life". What really happened in those five months he never publicly explained, and indeed he later invented a journey to Mexico "to map the ruins in Yucatan" to cover these missing months. He allowed this story to gain currency through an interview in 1932, he repeated it to friends such as the journalist Ivor Brown, and it was still being repeated in literary publications as late as 1990. Whether some traumatic event occurred in this period will never be known, although a quarrel with Rebecca, if it took place, would have been devastating enough. It is more likely that nothing at all happened: that he lodged in some anonymous room in London and tried to write, but could produce nothing of any quality or value. This dark period and his decision to rejoin the armed forces formed the third such crisis in his life, when he found himself unable to shape his life in the way that he wished. But now he was clear-sighted and philosophical: he had to live, and he determined to work conscientiously at his job, and to devote his private energies to writing. In January 1924, five months after entering the RAF he wrote to an old friend from Aberdeen, reflecting on his recent life:

> I believe it lies in me even yet – faith in the belief that I'll yet write something worthwhile. Except in details, I imagine the essential things in life have altered very little for me in the last five years. Only – actually – I believe I've gathered a sense of humour!

After initial training at Uxbridge, Mitchell was posted to RAF Kenley in Surrey. No foreign travel was involved with the RAF at that period, he was not a trainee flyer, and his job would be purely clerical. He maintained his socialist beliefs, but to have overtly campaigned for communism would have cost him his job. His writings contain several references to the General Strike of 1926 for example, and there is no doubt where his sympathies lay; but he can have taken no active part in those events. He was resigned to studying and waiting: he was after all still only in his mid-twenties. Having been starved of books in the army he resumed his researches, mainly into ancient history and social thought, and spent many hours in the British Museum among the antiquities and in the reading room. Early in 1924 he and Rebecca Middleton met again. Whatever had or had not passed between them in the previous year was put behind them. He sent her a telegram asking her to meet him outside the British Museum. She did so, and from that time onwards their relationship was unbroken. He was living in quarters at RAF Kenley, she in lodgings in west London. His off-duty time was spent with her or in writing. In *Stained Radiance* and *The Thirteenth Disciple* Mitchell has left pictures of that period, of hesitant romance in cheap lodging houses, of flirtations with artistic or political fashions, of the pervading disillusionment of post-war society, and of total uncertainty about his identity and about the future.

In autumn 1924 that uncertainty was lessened slightly by the appearance of his first work in print, a short story entitled 'Siva Plays the Game' which he entered for a short-story competition in the magazine *T.P.'s & Cassell's Weekly*, a lively journal of literature and book reviews. His story won the competition and it was published on 18 October 1924, with the judges' glowing words "In Mr Mitchell has been found a new author with a future before him as a writer of short stories". The story is set in Egypt and relates a deception practised on a naive English writer who cannot distinguish fantasy from reality. The style is mannered, and its theme is slight enough, but its importance lay in the fact of its publication, and the encouragement it gave to Mitchell to continue writing. Only the rejected writer knows the wounding sense of failure that comes with the experience of manuscripts rejected, whereas the published author has broken through a psychological barrier, and where he has succeeded once, he knows he can succeed again.

He was writing poetry throughout this period, and submitted it to literary journals such as *The London Mercury*, but without success. Some of his poems clearly drew upon his Middle Eastern experiences and on his passion for ancient history:

> I have drunk deeply of the ancient wine,
>> Wandered a summer in the Sumer land,
> Heard in the dusk the bells of Cretan kine
>> And maidens' song across the Cnossan strand...

While others reached back to memories of Eastern Scotland:

> ...quieter than a dream of summer days,
> Death comes into the russet, fruitful land:
> When out against the windy skies of eve
> A lap-wing wheels with wild and eery call,
> And in the fir-wood's fern-strewn fortresses
>> The sunset's shadows fall.

These poems are in a way accomplished enough, and they make their point, but their voice is mannered and dated: they might have been written by a minor Victorian poet half a century before. Mitchell must have believed that poetry meant stepping outside one's real life, and assuming a deliberate nobility of language, imitated from classical models. He could not apparently see it as springing directly from life or from the self, and finding an authentic voice for twentieth-century realities. He wrote more stories and ultimately he wished to write novels, although he did not attempt one until he began work on *Stained Radiance* in 1927. After the initial excitement of the success of 'Siva Plays the Game' came the inevitable reaction: what after all did one short story in one magazine amount to? Not very much it seemed in the four years that passed between the appearance of 'Siva' and his next published work.

Leslie Mitchell had not returned to Arbuthnott since the crisis of 1919, but in June 1925 he and Rebecca decided to revisit their families. Their motive may have been partly to announce their relationship, possibly even their engagement. They travelled by boat from London to Aberdeen and spent two weeks in the Mearns. Mitchell's parents were cool with him, as they always were, Rebecca's more welcoming. This journey to Arbuthnott and two others in the next five years started a process of re-awakening in his mind: he began unconsciously to re-evaluate the rural community, and the pattern of his own life since he had left it. His intimacy with Rebecca, who shared this background with him, became an important part of that process. Whether they had been lovers before this time is unknown, but it seems certain that they were lovers during this trip, and soon after their return south they were married at Fulham Registry Office on the 15 August 1925. Rebecca was later informally re-christened with the Greek Rhea which in turn became shortened to Ray. They celebrated their wedding-day by buying a typewriter, Mitchell's symbolic statement of faith that their joint future lay in his writing.

Rebecca Middleton was unquestionably the most important person in Leslie Mitchell's life. From his youth he sought intellectual answers to life's enigmas, but he needed personal love too, and his immediate family could not or would not give it. His relationship with Ray was a great healing influence in his development. Of her life and character

"In the ley field old Bob stood with his tail to the wind."

there is virtually no direct, recoverable record, yet she has a unique memorial in his works. Mitchell clearly had in his mind an ideal image of a woman who appears again and again in his books, from Thea Mayven in *Stained Radiance* to Chris Guthrie, a woman who is sensitive and intuitive, yet cool and self-contained, a woman who is wholly and instinctively involved in life's processes of love and suffering, but who preserves some inner core of selfhood that is hers alone. Those who knew Ray closely sensed that this figure was modelled on her, and one of the reasons that *A Scots Quair* is incomparably Mitchell's best book is that it is partly her book too. The adoption of her voice and her persona freed him from the obsessive themes of his own mind, and compelled him into a more sensitive and more authentic vision. Her personality was a vital catalyst in his creative processes.

Yet this was in the future, and the months following their marriage were tragic ones. It is possible that Ray was already pregnant when they married: if not, then she became pregnant very soon afterwards.

Under the absurd rules of the time, she was compelled to give up her job in the civil service when she married. They lived in Kenley near Mitchell's RAF base, in a succession of sordid rooms. Ray herself remembered these months as a time of horror and misery. In January 1926 Ray lost her baby and was near to death with eclampsy. The description of Thea's near-fatal illness in *Stained Radiance* is not fiction, it is not even literature: it is Mitchell's expression of the concentrated anguish of that period, and of his guilt as the cause of Ray's illness. He wrote to her "I knew myself as your murderer...and I asked you darling not to die." The same experience was relived, with slightly less intensity, more than four years later in the short story 'Daybreak' and it left its mark on *Cloud Howe*.

Ray survived, and went first to Devon to recuperate, then back alone to the Mearns for several months, where Leslie joined her in June. The first year of their marriage had been a traumatic one of near-poverty, sickness, guilt and separation. Yet their relationship not only survived but was strengthened. It is remarkable that they had known each other for 17 years at the time of their marriage; that they had grown closer so slowly as they had grown to maturity. In a very real sense, they had always shared each others' lives, had the same roots, the same childhood, and now the same exile in London. During the months of separation from Ray in 1925, Mitchell composed a sonnet called *The Lovers* in which he celebrates the experience of rebirth:

> The thousand lamps of the stars shall be ours,
>   And the wind's voice singing, and the sun's light,
> Music of earth shall haunt our dreaming hours.
>   We'll sleep and wake, turn in the kindly night,
>
> Each unto each, and know the other there,
>   And kiss in dreams and sleep with even breath:
> We've paid to peace in pain and sick despair,
>   We've made to Life the sacrifice of Death.
>
> We shall pass on: of those we shall forget
>   In the press of years, in newer sadness.
> Yet sometimes, when the lights of night are set,
>   Then shall we remember them with gladness,
>
> For that they gave, and bring in tears again,
>   The love that makes our hearts remember then.

Although clearly inspired by the sonnets of Christian Rossetti, this is a remarkably tender tribute to his wife, and a statement of faith in their future together after such a tragedy. The importance of this personal experience for Mitchell's thought was profound, for it darkened his view of the forces which shaped human life. Even more than the things he had seen in Glasgow, this transformation of the experience of birth into one of near-death convinced him that a random disorder, at times so destructive that it resembled a demonic malevolence, was inherent in the created order, and that man's inhumanity was merely one expression of it. Many of his earlier books contain passages where a language of violence and suffering is unmediated by any literary art: it attacks the reader, as Mitchell felt that the cruelty inherent in the world attacked its victims. The sources of this intuition must have lain deep in his own personality, but it was sharpened in those traumatic months of 1926.

In July 1926 Mitchell and Ray returned south together. He was transferred to RAF Uxbridge and they found rooms in Angel Road, Harrow, from where Mitchell cycled each day to work. They were effectively making a new beginning to their married life. Ray was not able to find other work and financially their lives were extremely basic as he settled down in a concentrated attempt to write. For a man in his position this was a tremendous act of will, requiring of him integrity and determination to give expression to the insights and conflicts of his personality. It is not surprising that his early writing shows great artistic uncertainty. From the late summer he wrote a number of new stories, often using Middle East themes as the background. He must have felt keenly that he was writing very much in literary isolation. The literary coteries of the 1920s and 1930s have been very fully investigated and described by historians, especially the degree to which the participants were interrelated. The writers, editors and artists who shared the same background of public school and Oxbridge, married into each others' families and went on to share the Bloomsbury, Garsington, country-house and foreign travel circuit. To these people writing was a natural activity, and with their contacts among editors and publishers it could also be a worthwhile occupation. Mitchell was completely outside of this kind of network. He was not part of a circle of intellectual friends; he had no contacts in

the literary establishment of London. He had no university background, no influential friends who were publishers or critics, no
private wealth. It is true that without these things he might still have
entered literary society, but he had not the brilliance of Shaw or the
fierce self-confidence of Lawrence to achieve that. And that was not
what he wanted: he was at this time an essentially private man
seeking a public voice, and until he found it Ray was his only
confidante. In his uncertainty he decided to send one of his stories to
several friends and to ask their frank opinion of it. One of those
selected was Alexander Gray, with whom he had remained in contact.
The story was 'The Ten Men of Sodom' (later renamed 'For Ten's
Sake'), a melodramatic tale of hatred transformed into forgiveness.
All the four friends thought it a powerful story and Mitchell began
sending it to magazine editors for possible publication. The results
were bitterly disappointing, but its rejection had important consequences:

> Ray and I laid our heads together. Could I write or could I not? Was I
> merely boring an over-weary world? We would put the matter to test and
> send the *Ten Men* to some noted author for his opinion. Mr H. G. Wells
> was selected as victim. Probably his secretary would return it without
> remark. No matter. Mr H. G. Wells was unexpected. He wrote personally
> on April 4th. 'Very good story' wrote the great H. G. from Olympus.
> 'Stick to it! You can do this sort of thing and will certainly come through'.

Mitchell was understandably thrilled by this judgement from a
writer of Wells' stature, but still no editor would publish the story.
1927 passed still in literary isolation, but he worked unremittingly on
new subjects, including a speculative book on exploration and he
began his first novel. Like many other unsuccessful writers, he toyed
with the idea of buying a small printing-press and producing his
works himself. He even experimented with writing thriller stories,
purely with the aim of getting into print. In 1928 he and Ray were
separated again when he was stationed at Upavon in Wiltshire with
leave only one weekend in three. This posting did at least provide him
with the opportunity to visit the most famous archaeological site in
Britain, Stonehenge, which was only ten miles away, and he used this
area as the setting in his later novel *Gay Hunter*. He and Ray had
moved several times in West London, settling finally in a ground-floor

Bennachie's ridges.

flat in Percy Road, Hammersmith which became their home for two years. It had few comforts, but Mitchell was largely indifferent to his surroundings. He had been promoted to corporal, making their finances slightly easier, but the only fulfilment which he sought still eluded him. Ray always maintained her belief that he could write successfully, and knowing that he would never be at peace until he could prove himself as a writer, she became anxious at his failure to find a publisher. In March 1928 on her own initiative she sent 'The Ten Men of Sodom' with the H. G. Wells letter to the editor of the *Cornhill* magazine, one of the most solid literary journals. To their delight the editor, Leonard Huxley, accepted the story and invited Mitchell to submit more work in the same vein. Almost simultaneously his study of exploration was accepted for publication by Kegan Paul, as part of their series of polemical essays called *Today and Tomorrow*, a series for which Bertrand Russell and Robert Graves, among others, had written. At this date the *Cornhill* was a far from exciting literary journal, and the seventy-year-old Huxley, father of Aldous and a member of one of the most eminent intellectual families in Europe, was conscious of its great days as publisher of Thackeray, George Eliot and Hardy. Nevertheless Mitchell was understandably excited by this breakthrough. In December 1928 Mitchell met Leonard Huxley at the *Cornhill* offices, and afterwards reported joyfully to Ray that Huxley had commissioned a series of Middle Eastern stories from him, and that he had therefore decided to leave the RAF when his six-year term ended the following summer, and to write full-time. Ray's personal support and Huxley's professional judgement were crucial as he approached another turning-point in his life. But this time it was not a crisis of failure or loneliness, but a determined decision to trust to his own resources, both to live and to articulate the themes and the vision which had been maturing in mind since his childhood.

The first *Cornhill* story appeared in January 1929, and on 31 August of that year he was free of the RAF and became a professional writer. Despite the uncertainties of such a life, the long-delayed achievement of his intellectual independence gave a new sense of purpose and fulfilment to the tragically brief space of life which remained to him. His belief in himself and his determination to shape his own life would be justified, but at a cost which neither he nor Ray could possibly foresee. The outward events of his life were unremarkable from that time onwards. Living first in London then in Welwyn, his family life was, unusually for a writer of genius, exceptionally stable and fulfilling. He did not travel abroad, or indeed travel anywhere except on holiday to Eastern Scotland. He did not identify himself with political or intellectual causes, and he suffered no intense new personal relationships. He wrote obsessively, indeed the pace at which he forced himself to work undoubtedly contributed to his early death. His development was all inward, shaping his ideas and refining his means of expression through the seventeen books which he published. But this progress was not a smooth or logical one, for in Mitchell there were several contradictory forces at work, forces which deceived him or diverted him from his authentic vision. The story of his career as a professional writer is one of experiment and failure, of finding his true voice through the experience of exile and homecoming. He set out to create for himself a new identity, one that was intellectual, English, creative and independent. I₁ a sense he succeeded: he spent the rest of his brief life as a professional writer and advanced his personal philosophy of human history. In this he achieved something remarkable for a man of his background. But the success of that persona was fragile, and time has effectively destroyed it. Yet a deeper current of his personality found expression in another persona and with another language, in which his vision achieved something authentic, unique and permanent.

Chapter 3   The Professional Writer:
Failure and Fulfilment

In *Cloud Howe* we meet briefly the wife of a farmer whose son "lived in London and wrote horrible books". This was Mitchell's ironic self-portrait, written because he knew what his family felt about his books and his way of life. And today, to the reader who knows only *A Scots Quair*, the discovery of Mitchell's other books is indeed a strange, puzzling and often disappointing experience. They not only inhabit a very different world from the *Quair*, but they seem to have been written by a different man. This strange dichotomy is both literary and biographical, and it reaches into the heart of Mitchell's life as a writer. These books other than the *Quair* reveal the paths which he deliberately took away from his origins, away from Scotland, and away from his self. His life and mind cannot be understood without a study of these books.

It was in 1927 and 1928 that Leslie Mitchell was writing the earliest of his published works – *Hanno, Stained Radiance* and the *Cornhill* stories, which were later published in book form as *The Calends of Cairo*. The outward routine of his life was mundane enough, that of an RAF corporal employed in clerical work. Of his intellectual development during these formative years we have no detailed knowledge. We know that all his private time was spent reading and writing, struggling to erect a conceptual framework for his perceptions of history and society. But precisely what he was reading, what were the models which guided him, his consciousness of contemporary literature, the kind of writing he wished to achieve – all these emerge only from the works themselves. Although his background was unusual, and although he was working in personal isolation from literary groups, he was clearly if unconsciously involved in the intellectual climate which shaped the literature of the 1920s.

The transformation of Victorianism into modernism involved most

"The sailing cloud-shapes over the Howe."

essentially a new awareness of human destructiveness and irrationality. The deceits and hypocrisy of social life had been attacked by Edwardian writers such as Shaw, Wells and Forster. But after the Great War, the analysis of social relationships alone no longer satisfied imaginative writers. The trauma of the war itself, the futile sacrifice of nine million lives, seemed to have revealed levels of barbarity from which Europe believed it had emerged centuries before. Post-war society was not cleansed or strengthened by the experience: it was haunted and crippled. A historic decline in western culture was sensed, a sickness in the human condition. The revolutionary insights of Freudianism and the philosophy of existentialism dissolved the old certainties about ourselves and our gods. Eliot's *Waste Land*, with its disturbing images of a fragmented culture, was the crucial literary document of the period. Among writers and artists there was a conscious search for new creeds and systems on which to build aesthetic or social programmes. To some the only response was social commitment, either to a new era of social justice, or to a vision of a strong, hierarchical society. To others the heart of the problem was man's dislocation from his true self, to which the only answer was a new subjectivity, to distinguish true selfhood from that which society shapes and controls. The perceived bankruptcy of the European governments that had pursued the war encouraged the growth of radical politics, and among many intellectuals and writers some form of communism was widely believed to be the key to the future.

The first two novels which the young Leslie Mitchell wrote, *Stained Radiance* and *The Thirteenth Disciple*, clearly inhabit this world of anxiety, dislocation and search. Yet there is also a very different element arising from the literary inheritance which Mitchell brought to his early writing. Like many first novels, they are strongly autobiographical, not merely in a narrative sense but in their revelation of intellectual influences. From Wells he had learned the concept of the break-out novel, where a working-class man throws off the fetters of a dead-end life; and from the adventure writers of his childhood such as Rider Haggard he had learned such symbols of quest as lost cities, or the transcendent personality whose identity is linked to some deeper destiny. It is the construction of his novels from these widely different frames of reference – post-war anomie and escapist adventure – that gives Mitchell's early books their strangeness. When his favourite themes of revolutionary socialism or anthropology are added, some of the slightly later books, such as *Three Go Back* or *The Lost Trumpet*, verge on fantasy or fable.

His first published work, *Hanno, or the Future of Exploration*, is a slight book, an essay in quasi-scientific prophecy in the manner of H. G. Wells. Mitchell foresaw the use of the helicopter and the submarine to push back the boundaries of the unknown. But then his imagination took over as he predicted the exploration of the earth's interior and of space. The book is an intriguing record of some of the scientific, or pseudo-scientific, theories which were current in the 1920s – about a world beneath the earth's crust, about life on Mars, and so on. This book's main interest for the study of Mitchell's life is the amazing breadth of reading it displays: the book claims an intimate knowledge of the literature and technology of astronomy, anthropology, archaeology, geology, exploration and survey. On the evidence of this book, unless Mitchell took short-cuts via popular encyclopedias, his life must have been centred obsessively on books, spending countless hours endlessly reading.

Hanno was written to a publisher's brief, but Mitchell's next book was his first expression of his own mind and personality. *Stained Radiance* is not an easy book to read or enjoy. It struggled long and hard to find a publisher, and even Ray Mitchell disliked it on a personal level, suggesting that its characters "want scouring and hung out to get some good fresh air". It may be that Ray was also disturbed to see their own lives so clearly exposed in book form. Nevertheless it is an important book for it offers a window on its author's inner life, and it prefigures a number of important themes in his mature work.

The first part of the book introduces a disparate group of young people in London, brought together by life in rented rooms in Chelsea. Some are committed communists, some are mere pleasure-seekers; all are disillusioned, unfulfilled, adrift in the post-war wasteland. The two central figures are portraits of Mitchell himself and of Ray: John Garland, a would-be novelist, embittered and rootless, and Thea Mayven, tormented because she belongs neither in London nor in her Scottish home. Sensitive but contained, Thea's innate nobility prefigures that of Chris Guthrie, and her relationship with Garland is transparently based on Mitchell's feelings for his wife. Thea herself excepted, the sterility of these people's lives is mirrored in the mirthless, sardonic quality of the writing: the characters are presented almost as pathological specimens, incapable of love, joy or creativity. A visit by Garland and Thea to her Scottish home in the "Leekan Valley" introduces a new dimension of vitality to their relationship, and they become lovers. The book comes to life here, the writing is more direct and authentic. But the lovers cannot remain in the Leekan Valley; the emotional conflicts of Thea's childhood are still too strong, and the peasant life is not for them. They return to London, marry and re-enact the nightmare of Ray's pregnancy and near-death. When the book ends Garland is clear-sighted in his hatred for the "Walls of the World"; for him the healing power of personal love alone is not enough.

Like many first novels, *Stained Radiance* fails because it attempts too much. Mitchell wished to write both a novel of ideas and an essay in social realism. The influence of Lawrence and the psychology of the

"A land grown desolate against its changing sky".

unconscious is visible too in the book's handling of sexual liberation
and the discovery of the self as he explores the problem of personal
liberty in a shattered world. Post-war disillusion and personal anomie
is rendered through some passages of interior monologue, where inner
and outer worlds merge. Mitchell had probably read Joyce's *Ulysses*,
but he was not really at ease with such technical experiments. The
most prevalent style in the book is a heavy irony, which Mitchell had
learned from the novels of Anatole France. But irony is a dangerous
technique on which to base a novel. It involves the writer in
distancing himself from his material, and assuming a façade of
omniscience. To the reader it can appear that the author is
manipulating the whole drama in order to demonstrate his cleverness.
It can have a deadening effect, and Mitchell's fondness for irony
devitalised much of his writing, fiction and non-fiction. On both the
narrative and stylistic levels, Mitchell's art in *Stained Radiance* is not
equal to what is being attempted, and the book fails through a lack of
clarity and vitality. It achieved some notoriety as a controversial

book, but then as now, no publicity is bad publicity and Mitchell was not displeased with the response. H. G. Wells wrote to him personally praising the book.

The first fruits of Mitchell's freedom from the RAF were his second novel *The Thirteenth Disciple*, and the extended series of stories published in the *Cornhill* magazine. These stories played an important, if negative, part in Mitchell's development as a writer. On a scale smaller than the novel he was able to experiment with ideas, characters and descriptive prose. He also gave expression to certain personal themes – eastern exoticism, melodrama, religious symbolism – to which he was to return in the future. The resulting stories are highly mannered in style and subject, and the human dramas contained in them are quite unconvincing. His attempts to reproduce in English the idiomatic speech of his exotic characters are artificial and distracting to the reader. Some of the dramatic narrative passages are so mannered that one is left uncertain as to what has actually happened. Yet Mitchell himself retained a high regard for them and when they appeared in book-form he dedicated them to his parents. He seems to have felt that he was working a literary tradition of exotic adventure and scene-painting, seen in such writers as Bulwer Lytton and Rider Haggard, yet the obvious theme inherent in such settings – the conflict between western and oriental values – he did not explore.

His second novel, *The Thirteenth Disciple*, was published in January 1931. Its early chapters are the most directly autobiographical things he ever wrote, drawing on his crofting childhood and the traumas of his young adulthood, while the latter part of the book presents what was probably the most important intellectual event in Mitchell's life, his discovery of diffusionism. Since settling in London in 1923, Mitchell had spent many hours in the British Museum, and his intensive researches into anthropology became a decisive influence on his writing. His long-held interest in prehistoric man had its roots in his childhood imagination, his curiosity about the people who had hunted or farmed in the Mearns before even the Romans came to Britain. Since then he had read widely around the whole subject and had seen some of the ancient sites of the Middle East. Yet his ideas and intuitions about early man did not become fully focused until he discovered, towards the end of the 1920s, the theories of the diffusionist school of anthropology, which centred around Grafton Elliott Smith, a professor at University College, London. Mitchell took his own researches extremely seriously, and introduced himself to Elliott Smith by letter. After a bad start, they developed a relationship of mutual respect, and Elliot Smith had a high regard for Mitchell's thought and writings.

The main tenets of diffusionism were twofold: first, contrary to the accepted view that civilisation had evolved simultaneously all over the world as part of the natural progress of early man, diffusionism taught that civilisation had come into being at a specific date in ancient Egypt, and had diffused throughout the rest of the world. This aspect of diffusionism was a matter of scholarly debate over archaeological evidence, over cultural sources and processes. The second principle of diffusionism was more a matter of subjective interpretation: it was that the institutions of civilisation – laws and religions, power and kingship – were corruptions of man's innate character, that there had been a golden age before men were enslaved to false gods, false codes, and the quest for power and wealth. The force of these two leading ideas came as a revelation to Mitchell, focusing his intuitive sense of history as a nightmare from which he was trying to awaken. Here was an insight into the paradox which had tormented him since childhood – why people who might be free and noble were enslaved by work, greed and brutality. It put into perspective the harsh labour of crofting, the slums of Glasgow, and the barbarism of war. It explained above all his divided self, the alienation he had felt from his family, from his fellow soldiers, and from the wasteland of London. His intuition of a richer, nobler life he could now identify as a biological memory, which is buried in all of us, of this lost golden age. And it did not merely explain the past, it pointed the way to the future, to the restoration of the golden age, achievable only through social revolution. One aspect of diffusionism which struck Mitchell very forcibly was that agriculture lay at the heart of this primal fall from innocence: it was the annual flooding of the Nile, and the consequent growth of crops, which prompted the ancient hunters to settle and cultivate the land, and all the evils of hierarchical society followed from that event. Mitchell's own bitter memories of his crofting childhood now appeared to him to be a re-enactment of that far-distant tragedy.

This theory has all the hallmarks of a substitute religion, a secular faith. It has a heaven, a fall from grace, and a hell. But being supposedly based only on the realities of history, it has no god. Mitchell always described himself as a rigorous materialist, yet his veneration of the lost golden age is uncannily like the Platonic doctrine that knowledge is recollection: recollection from a higher state of being from which man has become separated. Mitchell was, in an undirected sense, a very religious man, but one who could never find his god. The significance of the title *The Thirteenth Disciple* is precisely that in the gospels there was no thirteenth disciple: he was a phantom, was the unlucky one whom Christ never called, was Mitchell himself. He habitually described religion as archaic science, a concept which he learned from the great pioneer anthropologists Sir Edward Tylor and Sir James Frazer, who had interpreted magic and witchcraft among primitive peoples as pseudo-science. But now, having rejected religion, he believed he had found an intellectual key which he felt could interpret the chaos of history. In *The Thirteenth Disciple*, Malcom Maudslay (the name is taken from that of the Mayan archaeologist A. P. Maudslay) re-enacts the progress of Mitchell's own life from a Scottish croft, to communist activity in Glasgow, the army, and postwar London. Like John Garland, he is rootless and embittered and personal love alone cannot satisfy him. But unlike Garland he discovers a secular faith on which to build his life. At the climax of the book, Maudslay, lost in the Mexican forest, sees but does not reach a lost city, which is both an intellectual symbol and a childhood memory of his reading of Rider Haggard's adventure stories.

Like many young writers Mitchell used his first works to analyse his life, and to exorcise a number of ghosts. His sense of anger and alienation, accumulated over many years, pervades his early work, poisoning his prose with images of violence, suffering and despair. This dark side of his work had origins deep in his mind, and it never entirely lost its power over him. One reviewer commented on his "ineradicable habit of pausing in his narrative to insult everything and everyone in the universe". Like so many of the faults of his early books, this lack of control springs from a fundamental uncertainty about where to place the authorial voice. Was he trying to write realistic novels inhabited by convincing, living people? Or novels of ideas and ironic social analysis? Or confessional novels of his own inner life? What exactly was he trying to achieve? He could not have given a clear answer to that question, and that lack of clarity explains the stylistic uncertainties. There was also the problem of his prose. From an early age Mitchell had shown a precocious mastery of language, and he had cultivated a mature style based on literary models. But for books about inner conflicts which he was now writing, this style was not subtle or flexible enough. Instead it was overwritten, parading its own cleverness before the reader.

As Mitchell must have been aware, these novels lacked vitality because the conflicts within his characters lacked conviction. With the discovery of diffusionism he saw the possibility of using its concepts as a framework around which to build his novels, a framework which would give narrative drive, and set up a balance of forces which would bring the novels to life. Over the three years 1932-34 he published five novels in which the evils of civilisation are shown in contrast to man's nobler primitive nature. Three of these books (*Three Go Back, The Lost Trumpet*, and *Gay Hunter*) are imaginative fables, with elements of Wellsian prophecy on the one hand, and of the religious fantasies of C. S. Lewis on the other. They involve foreign exploration, time-travel, the discovery of Atlantis, and religious symbolism, both pagan and biblical. The metaphor of quest is present in all of them, and their theme is self-discovery through intellectual search and personal love. *Image and Superscription* was written immediately after *Stained Radiance* but not published until March 1933. It is another spiritual autobiography, in which the repressive forces of religion and corrupt secular power are in conflict with the insights of diffusionism and it contains some of Mitchell's most venomous anti-religious writing. The most distinctive of these books is *Spartacus*, a historical drama of the slave revolt in Rome in 73-71 B.C. It is the starkest of these books, for its ideas and its philosophy are transmuted into action, often swift and violent action. The cruelty of the master-slave relationship drew from Mitchell some of his typically brutal writing. Even friends and admirers criticised this tendency, but his reply was simple:

"The growth and ripening of that autumn's corn."

Yes, horrors do haunt me. That's because I'm in love with humanity. Ancient Greece is never the Parthenon to me: it's a slave being tortured in a dungeon of the Athenian law-courts; ancient Egypt is never the Pyramids: it's the blood of Goshen: Ancient Scotland is never Mary Queen: it's those serfs they kept chained in the mines of Fife a hundred years ago...

Mitchell's communist feelings are seen at their sternest in *Spartacus,* and the book shares with *Grey Granite* a meditation on historical destiny and on the sacrifice of the private life in the cause of intellect and belief. Mitchell's communism is articulate but its reality is elusive. He took no part in actiåe politics, but on the other hand it was not for him a mere temporary fashion, as it was for many other writers in the thirties. His communism was instinctive and visionary, an inevitable intellectual answer to the pervading injustice of the time.

In December 1931, just after the birth of their first child, a daughter, Rhea Sylvia, the Mitchells left London and moved to Welwyn Garden City in Hertfordshire. Welwyn had been founded in 1920 by Sir Ebenezer Howard, the second of his garden cities, which were a conscious attempt to reverse the drift of population to the major towns and to design a new environment for twentieth-century living. His ideas were in advance of any government thinking, and influenced urban planners throughout the world. The garden cities were built and owned by a private corporation and rented to the tenants. It has always been a source of perplexity that Mitchell, with his background and his mind, should have settled in Welwyn; the setting is felt to be incongruous for the author of *A Scots Quair*. Yet quite a number of artists and intellectuals were attracted by the garden city concept, and the population of Welwyn was more Bohemian than might now be imagined. And the simple truth is that Mitchell did not really care where he lived. The one certainty was that he could not live at peace in the North-East of Scotland. But beyond the desire for a room in which to write, and now a decent environment for his family, he was indifferent to his surroundings.

Mitchell's obvious satisfaction with his life in Welwyn offers an intriguing insight into his personality, and it raises the question of how he saw his outer life, how did he spend his time, when he was not writing, what was the fabric of his daily life? He did not travel; he never did explore England – or Scotland for that matter. He had no romantic enthusiasm for the countryside, and he had a positive dislike for anything resembling a tourist interest in palaces, castles or cathedrals. These institutions were to him symbols of corrupt power – the walls of the world. There is no record that he ever troubled to visit British cities, or the countryside for their own sake. It was only in the early 1930s on his journeys north, that he visited Edinburgh. His imagination was not visual, and he was, in this respect at least, the complete opposite of D. H. Lawrence, who travelled incessantly seeking an external setting that matched his ideal and his mood. Mitchell never expressed a desire to revisit the Middle East, or even Central America, which occupied his thoughts so much. Music and the theatre held no interest for him (he bought a gramophone in the last year of his life but his records were all of folk-songs) and he had no eye for art or architecture. He practised no sports. He was not actively engaged in politics at any level, and he was not taken up with any intimate relationships. He was apparently passionate exclusively about books and ideas, reading, questioning, seeking and writing. The collection of his books (now preserved in Edinburgh University Library) is a remarkable one for a creative writer in its concentration on history, archaeology and social theory: in aesthetics, even the aesthetics of literature, he apparently had no interest. This single-minded concentration lay behind his intellectual achievement, but there is no doubt that in a number of ways it also impoverished his creative work. So when the opportunity came to escape the world of rented rooms in London, he took it, and the family moved first to Edgar's Court, then to 107 Handside Lane, which became Mitchell's final home and the house in which *A Scots Quair* was written. A substantial house in a sheltered tree-lined street, in terms of comfort and style it is a world away from his origins in the croft of Bloomfield. Expatriation has been a powerful force in modern literature: Joyce's *Ulysses* is merely the most famous of the books written as an act of recall, over a distance of space and time.

Is it possible to sense what he was really like in this period as a man? Of average build and height, around 5′ 7″, his face was unusual: a high forehead with brown hair brushed straight back, and clear, pensive brown eyes. His long, curved nose was inherited from his father, the wide mouth from his mother. It was a calm face, but clearly the face of a man of ideas, of dreams and of some certainties, not least in himself. In the last year of his life he became thinner, perhaps through his illness, the face more aquiline and expressive. MacDiarmid thought he was gaunt, like an athlete stripped for battle. Like most men of his time he smoked heavily, but he was never a great drinker. He was generally a calm man, for he had spent years keeping his thoughts to himself, but his conversation could become animated, and he had a keen observation and an ironic sense of humour. In his twenties, in the services, ambitious but repressed and unsatisfied, he was ill at ease with many of his fellow men. Ray remembered his black moods during those years, and they were reflected in the fictional characters whom he created, who are restless and embittered. After he was freed of the army and the RAF, with the excitement of building his life as a writer, he became more sociable, and his personality opened out as he achieved success in his own terms. He was devoted to his family, and he began to enjoy some of the material things of life – his comfortable English home, a car, a gramophone – and he gained a wide circle of acquaintances, in Welwyn, London and Scotland. He was a leading figure in a Welwyn discussion group called The Twelve, who met frequently at his house. He was undoubtedly an opinionated man, a self-made man, who clung tenaciously to certain ideas and certain perspectives, which were the products of his background and of the intellectual journey he had made. Friendships were important to him, though with the exception of Alexander Gray, few went back to the years of his childhood or youth. Many were literary contacts from the years after *Sunset Song*, and the cordial relationships with people like Helen Cruikshank, James Bridie, or Neil Gunn were conducted entirely through letters. Some of these people met him only once or twice (some never met him) and have left impressions of his warmth and vitality. This was one aspect of his personality, but they had not known him during his years of struggle and uncertainty. He was a man in search of truth, yet, like many great artists, he was capable of a degree of self-deception, both in his life and in his writing. True intimacy was reserved always for Ray, with whom he had shared so much and who was so important for his creativity.

The reaction to his novels, after the controversy over *Stained Radiance*, was generally favourable. Elliott Smith himself wrote to say that *Three Go Back* had "rendered a useful service to those who are interested in clear thinking about human nature". Compton Mackenzie compared it to H. G. Wells and Jules Verne. An American edition was published and reviewed as "an adventure story for intelligent people, written by a man of science and a man of feeling". Sales of the first books were not high, but Jarrolds felt justified in accepting his subsequent work. Mitchell settled into a rhythm of intensive reading and writing. He was still very far from wealthy, but

"The sun poured in there, the tide whispered and splashed."

he now wrote so fluently and was so full of ideas that he was confident of the future. The only cloud on the horizon was the recurrence of a gastric illness, which he once described as feeling "as if a brood of rattlesnakes had taken up residence in my tummy". The seriousness with which he regarded his study of anthropology is clear from the stream of articles and books which appeared in parallel with his fiction, and the other works which he planned but never wrote. From articles on specific aspects of ancient history, he progressed to a full-scale study *The Conquest of the Maya*, 1934, and an even more ambitious "History of America Before Columbus", planned to run to 250,000 words, but never written.

Amid all this intellectual and literary activity, most strikingly absent was the Scottish dimension. In the years 1928-32, while he was building his secular faith and his literary career, Mitchell simply did not see himself as a Scottish writer. Yet we can now see that a slow process of emotional self-discovery was going on inside him. The years of alienation from his family, of servitude in the army, of intellectual despair, had yielded certain answers. He had found personal love with his wife and had achieved his ambition of writing professionally. He returned home to Bloomfield now each summer, and although the tension with his parents remained, his perspective on their world was gradually shifting. Something was ready to be released in him, a log-jam was ready to break up, so that he could confront the fundamental questions of his own life. Could his childhood world be reconciled with his mature view of history and society?

Sunset Song was written in the spring of 1932, and published in August of that year. It was immediately seen to be different in kind from his other books, indeed different from any other novel ever published, something both new and permanent in Scottish literature. It was *Sunset Song* that created for Mitchell the persona of a Scottish writer, strengthened exactly one year later by the appearance of *Cloud Howe*. If, after the publication of *Sunset Song*, Mitchell did not exactly wake up and find himself famous, it was still the most significant public event in his life to date. But he felt that it should have an impact on his private life too, vis-à-vis his family. He felt that its depiction of the fundamental nobility of peasant life would be recognised, and that his statement would act as a reconciling force between them. But his visit to the Mearns in the late summer of 1932 was deeply disappointing. His mother said to him:

> Laddie, what did you want to write all that muck for? You've the mind of a dirty midwife. It's the speak of the place, and I'm fair ashamed of ye.

The distance between Mitchell and his family could scarcely have a more graphic illustration than the gulf between the reconciliation he expected and this wounding rejection. He was deeply hurt, and it seems that Ray too now became included in his parents' disapproval, for sharing and encouraging his unconventional life. One wonders if Mitchell was aware of the Welsh writer Caradoc Evans, whose idiomatic and biting satires on Welsh rural life published between 1915 and 1935, made him "the most hated man in Wales". Mitchell's parents, like many other local people, noticed the satire in his book, but missed its deeper vision. Was he asking too much of them in expecting them to see the book with his eyes?

After *Sunset Song*, Mitchell was reviewed and discussed in private and in print by major Scots writers like MacDiarmid, Neil Gunn, and Compton Mackenzie. If he did not become close friends with them, he corresponded with them, was treated as an equal, and became, whether by choice or not, associated with the Scottish literary renaissance, indeed one critic considered that he had "put himself at the head of the Scottish revival in letters". Although he certainly did not drop his other major concerns, he saw the opportunity for further Scottish writing, and he was compelled to articulate for the first time his views on Scottish society, politics and culture. This overtly Scottish dimension and the writing that flowed from it after 1932 have given rise to a great deal of discussion about Mitchell's view of Scottish culture and politics. In particular it has been claimed that he would in time have inevitably come to support Nationalism. This must remain pure speculation, but all the evidence is against it. In the workshop of his mind, Scotland had become a new element, along with ancient history and socialism, but it is virtually impossible that it would have become dominant. Mitchell's own explicit statements support this view, and no creative writer, not even MacDiarmid himself, found in party-political Nationalism an ultimate resting-place.

The fruit of his new Scottish persona was the polemical work *Scottish Scene*, published jointly with Hugh MacDiarmid. The idea was Mitchell's and he planned the book's structure. He had admired MacDiarmid's work for some years and had met the poet in London during the early 1930s. In turn MacDiarmid was to write enthusiastically of *A Scots Quair* and *Spartacus*. MacDiarmid moved to Shetland before the two could become close friends, and the preparation of *Scottish Scene* was conducted entirely by letter. Each writer produced his contributions quite independently, and it is not in any sense a joint manifesto. Its publication was something of a sensation in Scotland, being received by press and public as a biting polemic on Scottish life and culture.

Mitchell's contribution was five short stories and seven essays. The stories, except the one entitled 'Forsaken', are written in the idiom of *Sunset Song*. 'Greenden' is the study of a haunted mind dissolving into madness; 'Sim' tells of the transformation of pride into bleak despair; while 'Clay' reaches into the heart of Mitchell's ambivalent feelings towards the peasant farmer – his poverty of mind and his nobility of character. The Mearns setting of these stories is totally realistic – hard, sharp and detailed. Yet at the same time they are full of the sense of another realm that exists beside this one, a realm of darkness, fear and despair. They are among the most powerful things Mitchell ever wrote, and it is almost incredible that they were written by the same man who, a year earlier, was writing the stilted melodrama of the oriental *Cornhill* stories. 'Smeddum' is lighter in style, but equally impressive, and one wonders if Mitchell was consciously exploring his feelings about illegitimacy, marriage and own parents' relationship.

The essays in *Scottish Scene* are Mitchell's only considered public statements on a whole range of aspects of Scottish culture, history and literature. They have been carefully studied in an attempt to discern his true feelings about Scotland, to resolve the ambiguities that are so evident in *A Scots Quair*. The most striking thing about these essays is that they are written in an elaborate literary prose utterly different from the language of the stories. They represent the traditional view that the essayist's art was to demonstrate the knowledge, even the omniscience, of the writer. Although there is humour, it is heavy and ironic; there is no lightness, no humility, almost no feeling in these essays. The most successful piece is 'The Land', where his willingness to trust more subjective insights, and a more flexible prose produced a statement that reveals something of the writer's true feelings. His holiday in the Mearns in the summer of 1933 lay behind this essay, when he explored the district on foot and by bicycle as he had twenty years earlier. It is revealing that he apparently never wished to take a holiday anywhere else, in Scotland or beyond.

There is some evidence that MacDiarmid himself was not entirely convinced by these essays, and he later pointed out that Mitchell's actual experience of Scotland was quite limited. He knew intimately only the farmland of the Mearns, and had lived briefly in Aberdeen and Glasgow, fifteen years before this book was written. He did not know Edinburgh, or industrial Scotland, the villages or market-towns, the Highlands or the Borders. To compose these essays, Mitchell drew on the impressions he formed before leaving Scotland: memories of Aberdeen and Glasgow, the kirk and the countryside, and his

"In that corridor of trees, the light fell dim."

readings of Scottish history, all re-interpreted in the light of his later ideas. If the attempt to claim Mitchell as part of the emerging sense of Scottish Renaissance or Nationalism rests on these essays, it must fail. He writes as clearly as possible of the historical "curse of small nations", and that "Scotland's salvation lies not in nationalism nor internationalism...but in ultimate cosmopolitanism". The ambiguity in Mitchell's feelings towards Scotland remain unresolved in these essays, and part of the problem lies in his style: in demonstrating knowledge, he evades commitment.

In the last full year of his life, 1934, Mitchell generated a virtual whirlwind of literary activity. In retrospect the most important event was the publication of *Grey Granite* in November, completing *A Scots Quair*. But Mitchell had no less than five other books published in that year: *Niger: the Life of Mungo Park*; *The Conquest of the Maya*; *Gay Hunter*; *Scottish Scene*, and *Nine Against the Unknown*. The future projects which he was planning were even more numerous: a study of the world's great religions; a biography of Wallace; a novel of the covenanting period; an autobiography; a new novel of the Mearns; a history of America before Columbus; and a comprehensive history of mankind. He wrote for eight hours or more each day, dividing it into blocks of 90 minutes, each devoted to the three or four works in progress. He spoke and wrote of his two writing identities as if they were two separate people. He referred to his two typewriters, one for the Scottish novelist, the other for his "English cousin". In his desire to sustain both identities, it seems that he planned literally two men's work: Scottish novels and Scottish history from the one, archaeology and philosophy from the other. There was something feverish and irrational in this ceaseless drive to produce book after book. It was as though he were haunted by the years of literary struggle and sterility in the 1920s, and had to ensure that they could never recur. It is striking too that he would not concentrate on novel-writing: he was never convinced that *A Scots Quair* was his masterpiece, and he was determined to achieve distinction as a historian and a thinker.

In pursuit of this aim, one of the most remarkable books Mitchell ever wrote was *The Conquest of the Maya*. Tracing the history of the people of Yucatan from c.3000 B.C. to their subjugation by the Spaniards, it is a work of serious and detailed research over which Mitchell took great pains. It provides striking proof of how much he had achieved through self-education: with no formal education beyond the age of 17, he mastered all the contemporary literature in this arcane field of knowledge, and produced a work of synthesis which Elliott Smith himself praised in glowing terms. For Mitchell the interest of the Mayan civilisation was that it provided, in his eyes, a classic demonstration of the cardinal point of diffusionist theory: that the marks of civilisation – agriculture, theology, warfare, and slavery – had originated in ancient Egypt and spread across most of the world, including to America via post-glacial landbridges. The point of the book is to warn that the brutality and warfare into which the Maya declined could also destroy twentieth-century man. At the heart of the book is an imaginative reconstruction of the life of the Mayan people, written by Mitchell in deliberate defiance of dry, academic history. It is a vivid and brutal portrait of the rulers and their slaves, the priests and their victims, displaying once again Mitchell's vicious use of language to attack the institutions of civilisation. This is an important book in the context of Mitchell's writing. The complex of ideas which motivated his work formed a unity in his mind: fiction and non-fiction were products of the same workshop, the same vision. Imaginative reconstruction of the past was what drew him to write his biography of Mungo Park, *Niger*. The opening chapters describing Park's farming childhood are pure autobiography, as Mitchell projects his own memories of alienation and escape into the world of books back onto his subject. These passages are directly comparable to the fictional biographies in *The Thirteenth Disciple* and *Image and Superscription*. The recurrence of this theme suggests that Mitchell really needed to write a genuine autobiography, one that was both objective and deeply-felt, but that he never found the necessary literary means. Perhaps this was fortunate, for he kept all his emotional energy to pour into the *Quair*.

Mitchell accepted the role of Scottish writer, and following the interest aroused by *Scottish Scene* he began to co-ordinate a series of books to be called "Meanings in Scotland", for which he invited figures such as Compton Mackenzie and Neil Gunn to contribute extended essays on subjects from religion to whisky. A. S. Neill was recruited to write on education, and through this contact Mitchell's son Daryll later went to Neill's progressive school Summerhill in Suffolk. Mitchell's range of correspondence with Scottish writers grew, though it cannot be said that he formed intimate friendships with them. The question of returning to Scotland inevitably arose, as Ray described:

> He was tempted to come back. We both were. One summer he went to Scotland to look at possible houses and at the same time to get ideas and inspiration. He came back much earlier than he intended. 'It's no use' he said, 'there's no inspiration for me up there. I would be too close to it all. This is where I can write about Scotland.' So we stayed in Welwyn...

Nevertheless each summer or autumn from the late 1920s onwards he and his family did return to the Mearns, and in September 1934 he made what was to be his last visit to his parents and to the valley of Bervie Water. He drove north, alone this time in his newly-bought car, because their son Daryll, born in March that year, was too young for the long journey. He spent some time in Edinburgh with the poet Helen Cruikshank, before travelling on to Kincardine. He intended to research both the planned covenanting novel and the Wallace biography. At Bloomfield, his literary successes had not reconciled his parents to his unorthodox life, the nature of the books themselves being no doubt partly responsible for that. But he had become more patient and understanding towards them, and his brother John noticed the new element of compassion in his feelings for them. Ray tried to sum up the ambivalence in their attitude towards him:

> They were proud of him and they were ashamed of him, and they never knew which was uppermost. Proud when the great names in the world spoke of his work with praise; ashamed when some neighbour was shocked at something in one of his books. That autumn Leslie acquired a car and drove them about. His mother was pleased and proud, but later he had a difference with his father. On the day of going away, Leslie went to say goodbye to him; they stopped at the top of the rig and looked at each other, the son full of sorrow, the father perhaps of bitterness, perhaps regret. 'Ta-ta father' said Leslie, and the only reply he got was 'Fine to be some folk, car and all. You're lucky to be able to afford it'. Leslie was deeply hurt.

So this final meeting between father and son was marked by bitterness and misunderstanding. Mitchell went on to visit his former teacher Alexander Gray, living now in Echt, and it was during his few days there that the final pages of *Grey Granite* were written.

After returning to Welwyn his last book *Nine Against the Unknown* was published. Strangely, it was, like his first book, a study of exploration from Leif Ericsson to Nansen, and the same quotation from Tennyson's *Ulysses* appeared as its epigraph. Those lines of Tennyson were displayed framed in Mitchell's study at his home. It is often claimed that Mitchell outgrew diffusionism after a few years, but the opening pages of this, his last book, contain a classic summary of the diffusionist view of history, and the bibliography is full of Elliott Smith and his disciples. In December he was seriously ill for two weeks with gastritis. He recovered in the new year, and took up his unremitting routine of work for some weeks, but he had so many projects in hand that he made little real progress with any of them. Did he realise how ill he was and refuse to face the fact? He did not apparently warn Ray, he did not make a will, and he had arranged no life insurance. With his brain teeming with literary plans, with his new-found fame, with his young family, how could either he or Ray

"The old stones rose up around her silently, some went back to the old, unkindly times of the Covenanters, one had a skull..."

have imagined the unimaginable? How far his illness was self-inflicted, caused by overwork, tension or financial anxiety, can never be determined. Quite suddenly he relapsed and became critically ill. Surgery failed to save him, and on 7 February 1935 Leslie Mitchell died in Welwyn Hospital. The cause of death was peritonitis following a perforated ulcer. He would have been 34 one week later. After cremation at Golders Green, in north London, his ashes were placed in Arbuthnott churchyard on 23 February. His wife and his parents, local people and literary friends, all shaken by the suddenness of the tragedy, gathered that day in the cold sunlight and tried to say goodbye.

Ray's first impulse was to return to Scotland, to a farm to reconstruct the life they had left behind. But she decided against it, and remained in Welwyn. She returned to work and began a long struggle to bring up her family and preserve the memory of her husband's work. Her tearless grief was like that of Chris Guthrie after the death of her husband. In the long years that followed, she learned to keep a great deal to herself, but the sense of the injustice of his death, at what was so ruthlessly taken from them both, was a wound which never really healed.

The story of the last six years of Mitchell's life is the story of his books. His outer life was uneventful, but he released a stream of creativity from his personality. In the years 1928-34 he found expression for the many conflicting forces in his mind, as he sought to hold in balance his ideas and his experience. Of the fourteen books written in these few years (counting the trilogy as one work) he achieved one acknowledged masterpiece, the writing of which occupied him in total for less than one year. What of the others which frame this achievement, how do they relate to *A Scots Quair*, and what do they tell us of Mitchell's mind and the pattern of his life? Mitchell's English books have their defenders, who argue that they are significant statements in their own right. Others say frankly that they are worthless, totally unrelated to the peak of Mitchell's achievement in the *Quair*. The truth is more subtle than either of these two extremes. The other books do indeed relate to *A Scots Quair* and they provide an essential framework for the understanding of Mitchell's life. Yet the defects of these books are all too clear, and there is little doubt that, were Mitchell's name not attached to them, none of them would be read today. The reasons for this literary failure are threefold – intellectual, aesthetic and biographical – and they take us close to the heart of the enigma of Mitchell's life.

Mitchell's English works are all essentially products of his intellect: they are records of his struggle to come to terms with the historical forces which he believed had shaped and corrupted human nature. He was seeking objective answers to universal questions, and in political and anthropological theory he believed he had found them. His English books were not rooted in a direct, instinctive perception of human experience. They were not written with compassion, insight or humour, nor out of an understanding of human integrity or weakness. They were written to present ideas, ideas of innocence, guilt, intellectual discovery, disillusionment, injustice; even love is brought into the narrative as an idea, a stage in intellectual growth. None of these things are presented to our senses, with the immediacy or vitality that is demanded by the subject. Mitchell himself was quite clear about this; he stated explicitly his belief that literature was propaganda, that the only rational motive for writing books was to advance ideas. Even his autobiography was planned as propaganda for his views on politics and history. In addition, there were a few fixed ideas, almost obsessions which recur in all his books: physical violence, religious tyranny, travel to the East or to Central America, and most obviously archaeology. It is the dominating presence of Mitchell's social and political ideas, together with the recurrence of these few personal symbols, which create a claustrophobia in the reader, a sense of being trapped in the writer's obsessions. Mitchell's equipment as a writer was formidable but it was flawed. He had intelligence, he had knowledge of literature, he had insight; but he had a serious lack of critical judgement of his own work. If his books embodied his dominant ideas, he was satisfied with them; criticism on any other grounds did not seem to concern him. For this reason he never acknowledged that *A Scots Quair* was on a different plane to his other work.

All this is perhaps another way of saying that Mitchell's English books have no true aesthetic sense. His language in these books does not satisfy the imagination: it has no sense of visual beauty and it has a comparatively restricted emotional range. Above all, it has no subjective dimension, able to present human experience directly to our senses. He does not enter the consciousness of any of the characters in these books; the presence we are constantly aware of is that of Mitchell himself. From his childhood Mitchell had longed to ''be a writer'', and he had cultivated a consciously literary style. He had also wished, like H. G. Wells, to be a polymath, to be able to handle any subject – history, biography, philosophy, and science – as well as fiction. But his prose, which he modelled on the Victorian classics, and on the academic sources from which he drew his history, produced a language that was heavy and inflexible. One is conscious all too often of the author's voice, expounding his ideas and manipulating his key images. Such a style robs his English novels of vitality. There is no atmosphere, no tension, no visualisation, no

shaping of significant detail. Most strikingly too, for the author of *A
Scots Quair*, there is no vestige of humour in any of these books; there
is heavy, self-conscious irony, but no humour. The essential strength
of the novel as an art form, its classical power of *mimesis* – the
imitation of reality – is missing.

These faults – over-intellectualisation and a weak aesthetic sense –
are all forgivable in a young writer, and may be written out in time.
But the third, and in some ways the gravest obstacle to Mitchell's
maturing as a writer, was biographical – the way he handled his
career. After the first title *Stained Radiance*, all his books without
exception were written with extreme haste. It is a matter of record
that he never revised his work; his surviving typescripts demonstrate
that while he changed a word or phrase, he never rewrote whole
passages, or cancelled or added sections. Certainly he did not rewrite
whole works in the way that D. H. Lawrence, E. M. Forster, Virginia
Woolf and many other writers did. Another curious fact is that all his
seven English novels are nearly the same length, slightly under
100,000 words each. The explanation for both these facts is that he
wrote for so many hours each day and produced a book every two to
three months. The result is that what we have are not finished,
considered works of art: they are spontaneous and uncorrected
records of his thought. Why did he write in this way? Simply to live.
Having invested three months in writing a work, he simply could not
afford to spend another three months revising it. Still less could he
afford to withhold it from publication altogether if it was unsatisfactory. This intense regime inevitably affected the quality of his
work; he came to see success as the mere completion and publication
of each book.

And yet the cruellest comment of all on this English work, fiction
and non-fiction, is that it was a financial failure. It is true that he
survived as a professional writer for just over five years, but the costs
were hidden, and they may have been fatal to him. After his death his
widow naturally contacted his publisher, Jarrolds, about the payment
of future royalties. The answer was devastating in its simplicity: the
only books likely to earn any future royalties were those published
under the Grassic Gibbon name – the *Quair*. On all his other books
there were "heavy unearned balances". It is clear that Mitchell had

"But that dark, hot cloud went by.... the dusky red of the harvest night."

relied exclusively on the advances on his next book, while the actual sales earned practically nothing. On his death his widow was left virtually penniless. Within weeks of his death she had to borrow money from friends, then return to full-time work. In subjecting himself to his punishing work schedule, Mitchell had gambled on the future, and the gamble failed. He believed he was building a firm literary career, but he was being driven into mere book-production, and none of these English books ever sold in worthwhile numbers, or was ever reprinted during his lifetime. On a deeper level too he was chasing illusions, for the diffusionist creed is now forgotten and Elliott Smith himself is a mere footnote in the history of anthropology. Mitchell's years of study and the labour he expended on books like *The Conquest of the Maya* had no value to anyone but himself. Hugh MacDiarmid later dismissed Mitchell's vision of history as a pipe-dream, unsupported by actual facts, and in this he was clearer-sighted than Mitchell himself. The reputation as a historian and philosopher of human nature, for which he worked so intensely, has vanished along with the whole school of thought of which he was a part. The self-imposed pressure of work has poisoned the lives of many writers. It ruined Compton Mackenzie as a serious writer, and it prevented Edward Thomas from becoming a major poet. But rarely can it have such tragic consequences as in Mitchell's case, for it almost certainly contributed to his early death.

His handling of his career is another demonstration of the strain of irrationality in his character. We ask why he could not have supported himself through outside work, and written more carefully, as Neil Gunn or Edwin Muir did. Many great writers have not hesitated to seek private patronage in their determination to pursue their art – it is known that James Joyce accepted thousands of pounds in private gifts between 1915 and 1935. But Mitchell's pride and ambition drove him to prove his independence from a society many of whose values he despised. He was impelled to justify his life in his own terms, by progressing from crofter's child and private soldier to professional writer. In the metaphorical sense books were his life, and he was determined to make them his life in reality too.

Yet these books were an essential part of the structure of his life. They record the inner journey which he had to undertake before he was ready to make his one unique statement. And finally he did achieve his ambition, and he wrote an incomparably great book. Yet it was not through intellectual discovery alone that he achieved his breakthrough, but through the re-discovery of a personal language which opened to him both a new human dimension and a new aesthetic sense. It was also an act of involuntary memory which gave him his vision. It was out of the context of the rest of his work, and it was not the work he had thought he wanted to write. He was not a writer who had believed in inspiration, yet when it came he had the integrity to accept it. Addicted to books, he made one great excursion from literature into life.

Chapter 4   Time Regained:
A Scots Quair

> I remember when he visited the Mearns that summer and we took a walk
> together. He was quick to notice changes – a new house built, an old one
> gone, some trees pulled down, a new fence started. 'It's changing John' he
> said. 'Aye Leslie, and it will change more' I replied. 'Why don't you write
> a book about it, about this place where you belong, and the folk round
> about? Then it will still be here when the folk are gone and more changes
> come.' 'I maybe will' he said. 'I maybe will'.

This is one story of the origin of *A Scots Quair*, told by Leslie
Mitchell's brother John. It is a good story, and John Mitchell was not
the only one who urged the writer to concentrate his mind on the
North-East, the region where he had been born and which had been
glimpsed in the background of his earlier books. Yet such suggestions
alone could not have produced a book as original and compelling as
Sunset Song. The historical, documentary aspect of the book, lucid
and forceful as it is, should not be allowed to obscure its psychological
structure. A complex process of inner development clearly lay behind
Mitchell's decision, settled in his Hertfordshire home in the spring of
1932, to begin work on his Mearns novel. He conceived it from the
outset as a trilogy of linked novels, larger in scope than anything he
had attempted before. It was to have both a personal and a historical
dimension: the central character was to re-enact man's historic path
through innocence and experience, joy and disillusionment, passion
and detachment. Yet Mitchell made three quite crucial decisions
before he began writing, decisions that were to distinguish this book
from everything else that came from his pen, and which created a
unique and wholly original work. These decisions concerned the
geographical setting of the work, its language, and its central
character.

Since his childhood, Mitchell had approached literature as an
escape from the confines of his everyday world into a deeper realm of
intellect and imagination. He himself deliberately left the place of his
upbringing when he was little more than a boy, and when he came to

write his books, all his leading characters act out his central theme of travel and self-discovery. Mitchell came very early in his life to see the world as a series of objective questions about civilisation, history and human society, and it seemed to him that the answers to those questions must lie outside himself and outside the narrow environment of his birth. Those answers must lie in study, travel, information, and exploration of the objective world. Therefore his decision to place a novel within the small, enclosed world of the Mearns was for him a radical step. But it was one which released in him a flood of subjective knowledge and impressions which he had never tapped before. His earlier novels were based on his hours of study in the field of anthropology, history and politics; but *Sunset Song* was the book he had been preparing all his life. All his intuition and his gift for observation could be given their freedom and create a mirror of reality which he had not previously approached in sharpness, clarity and authenticity.

The second and complementary decision which Mitchell took was to write this book in an idiomatic language that was totally new in the art of fiction, yet so apt for its subject as to appear natural, effortless and inevitable. We read it as a language we have known, heard and spoken for years, yet never before seen written down. Perhaps more than for any other time in Mitchell's life, we long for some personal account of his thinking and his motives – a diary, notebook, or other personal record that would reveal how he felt his way towards this new language. Before he wrote *Sunset Song* the quality of his prose had been one of the greatest flaws in his progress as a writer. In his English works, both fiction and non-fiction, it was too elaborate and self-conscious, always attempting to display too much knowledge and too much style; it was neither natural nor flexible. But in adopting the "rhythms and cadences of Scots spoken speech", Mitchell's language was transformed: it acquired both vitality and energy. It had both the subjective sensitivity to reach into the minds of his characters, and the objective power to present a scene or incident with miraculous clarity, hard, sharp and fully realised. It is as though the language and setting of the Mearns released in him all the pent-up creativity of a writer of genius, a hard narrative poetry that had until now been blocked or diverted into the pseudo-literature of his early works. This was the

"A cold little wind came by, she looked up and saw a thickening of clouds, rain-nimbus driving down."

language that had lain dormant in his mind for more than two decades, the language he had consciously rejected as a child.

This linguistic achievement is all the more remarkable when compared with the existing tradition of Scots vernacular fiction. Since the early nineteenth century, writers such as Scott and Galt had introduced a Scottish idiom into their novels, and this tradition was continued by Stevenson and Barrie. Yet none of these writers could apparently conceive any way of presenting Scots speech other than by phonetically-twisted English. This technique reached its height in William Alexander's *Johnny Gibb of Gushetneuk* (1871), a regional classic that has become the Bible of the North-East dialect, but whose very richness of idiom makes it almost impenetrable to the outsider. The other striking defect of this older tradition of Scots literature is its apparent schizophrenia: while the characters speak the broadest of dialects, the narrative passages are cast in an ornate, literary English. Indeed the English is so fastidious that one suspects the author of showing off his own virtuosity, his mastery of two languages. The effect of alternating between these two languages destroys any sense of dramatic reality in these books, and the characters become puppets.

Mitchell's solution to these problems was totally novel and totally successful. First he turns his back on phonetic Scots and gives us instead the structures and intonation of Scots spoken speech. With very little recourse to dialect words, his syntax and punctuation convey the pace and tone of the Scottish voice. Moreover, Mitchell discovered through the act of writing down this idiom that living dialogue does not take place in correctly structured sentences, but in a flow of phrases, questions, comments, claims, interjections, approval, laughter or insult. In his novel *Three Go Back* Mitchell's time-travelling heroine asks her primitive lover "I do hope you've some place in mind where we can shelter", and the narrator comments "Strange jargon in that Sunset Land!" This was Mitchell's prophetic insight that cool, correct, colourless English was utterly out of place in his imagined landscape, but while writing *Three Go Back* in 1931, he did not yet know what the answer would be. His second innovation was to place the authorial voice so close to the characters' voices that there is virtually no distinction between them. The narrative is as spontaneous and colloquial as the dialogue, and yet it is on occasion extraordinarily rich and poetic. Mitchell becomes the voice of the community and of the landscape, moving from character to character and from mood to mood, but also watching and interpreting the pattern of the drama. This sensitive placing of the author's voice was something that had eluded Mitchell in his other books, indeed his intellectual detachment, the sense of an author merely manipulating his subjects, is one of the principal reasons why those books lack conviction.

The third crucial decision about the nature of *A Scots Quair* was to adopt the persona of a woman, Chris Guthrie, on which to build the structure of the whole novel. The feminine ideal who had appeared in Mitchell's early fiction, now becomes the central focus. As D. H. Lawrence found, the adoption of a feminine persona gave both a freedom and discipline to his writing. There is no doubt that Chris's complex blend of sensitivity and pride, warmth and detachment was inspired largely by the character of Rebecca Mitchell. It was an act of genius for Mitchell to renounce the male authorial voice which had dominated his English books, and to create the *Quair* around Chris's personality, for which he had a living model. In this way he left behind many of his own obsessive intellectual concerns and stylistic faults. Chris Guthrie as a rootless intellectual, obsessed with archaeology and politics, would lack all conviction. Mitchell realised this, and he was compelled to enter her mind on her own terms, and to crystalise her world with a totally fresh objectivity. *Sunset Song* was set down with speed and intensity, and the experience of writing it generated in Mitchell a personal excitement that was new for him. He would read newly-written sections of it aloud to Ray and they would discuss it, conscious that it was their own life that was being recreated on the page.

Mitchell's awareness of the novelty and importance of what he had done when he finished writing *Sunset Song* was symbolised by his taking a new name under which to publish it. The suggestion of a pseudonym came from his publisher, Jarrolds, who rightly considered the book to be different from his earlier work, and who felt also that his enormous productivity might tend to devalue his reputation. The choice of the name was Mitchell's of course, and with it he paid his long-felt debt to his mother for the gifts which he was convinced had come from her, although his relationship with her was in truth scarcely less tense than that with his father. It is remarkable that the two foremost names in twentieth century Scottish literature, Mac-Diarmid and Gibbon, should both be pseudonyms, both taken to symbolise a new and specifically Scots identity.

These three vital decisions concerning the structure and character of his book lie behind the greatness of the *Quair*. How specifically did Mitchell use material from his own early life and from his later intellectual development to shape the trilogy? What did his painfully-formed ideas about human civilisation contribute to the *Quair*? How, after his long intellectual journey, did he now see the community of his birth, and his own early life there?

From the first lines of *Sunset Song* it is clear that this is a book like no other that Mitchell had written. In the vivid shaping of the novel's historical and geographical prologue, Mitchell is meditating on the context of his life, acknowledging that that context lies in the history, the people and the landscape of this small, enclosed community. This

"Winters or springs, summers or harvests, bristling or sunning the sides of Barmekin."

clearly-delineated framework has no parallel in his English novels, whose themes are travel and discovery, and where uncertainty rules. We know that Mitchell drew much of this historical material from his copy of J. C. Watt's book *The Mearns of Old*, and that he annotated the map in that book, locating Kinraddie just north of Arbuthnott, Segget midway between Drumlithie and Auchenblae, and Dundon (later changed to Duncairn) on the coast near Kinneff. It is significant that the house described as Blawearie bears a closer resemblance to the croft of Hillhead of Seggat than to Bloomfield. Within this closely-defined setting, the local figures are introduced each in turn like a gallery of portraits or a human comedy, perhaps a couple of dozen in all. These were clearly the people who inhabited Mitchell's childhood world, each strongly characterised as small, quick, mean, generous, lazy, skilful, quarrelsome, and so on. They are vividly seen, but not presented with any depth, not understood as people, and this is precisely how a child sees the adult figures who surround him. Those destined to play leading roles – Chae Strachan and Rob Duncan – are drawn with greater detail and humanity. This gallery of vivid, familiar figures contrasts strongly with the anonymous procession of city-dwellers in Mitchell's other books, and they evoke from him for the first time his strong comic sense, so long absent from his earlier writing. In a traditional community the roles that these people played were immensely important in defining their identity: their pride or lack of it, their authority or lack of it, stemmed from their role as farmer, minister, blacksmith, or seaman. As a child this had frustrated Mitchell because he needed to form his own personal identity, but he now saw these roles as capable of expressing vital human qualities.

We sense instantly that this world can be known and described only from the inside, and that the narrator is intimately acquainted with these people. Yet the three-part structure of prelude, narrative and epilogue which is used in every chapter of the *Quair*, serves to detach the central character from the action. The figure on the hillside, looking down on the town or village, recalling the past, stands somehow outside this world. This image is clearly drawn from Mitchell's boyhood memory of his hours on the hillsides around Bloomfield with a book, escaping from the world of his family and his schoolfellows. This detachment is apparent in the reiterated phrase "She saw clearly now..." or "Chris saw plain..."

Yet into this world comes the Guthrie family, and it is as though Mitchell is saying that behind the façade of these people's ordered lives is a darker and more complex pattern. It is clear that this family is not closely linked, not warm or emotional. There are deep tensions centred on the father's authority, on his religious and sexual repressions, and on the work ethic, the life of the farm. Each member of the family is locked in his or her own world and must love or suffer alone. Chris senses this darker dimension to their existence, and it is through her that Mitchell questions the forces that dominate their lives. For a time she escapes into the world of books and re-enacts the division in Mitchell's life between Scots and English values. But one of the key facts which underpins the whole of the *Quair* is that Chris is not driven to leave the North-East as Leslie Mitchell and Rebecca Middleton both did: she stays and lives a kind of alternative Mitchell-life as it might have been, acting out the inner conflicts of his character in his native region. The most striking symbolic event of this alternative life is that both parents die, freeing Chris to control her own life. There could be no starker image of Mitchell's alienation from his family than these retrospective deaths.

One of the many reasons that *A Scots Quair* is by far the richest of Mitchell's books, in both texture and humanity, is that he gives full weight to the irrational changes of thought and mood that are so characteristic of living people. One of the central moments of revelation in the whole trilogy is at John Guthrie's funeral when his daughter understands at last the nobility of his life:

> ...she minded then, wildly, in a long broken flash of remembrance, all the fine things of him that the years had hidden from their sight, the fleetness of him and his justice, and the fight unwearying he'd fought with the land and its masters to have them all clad and fed and respectable, he'd never rested working and chaving for them, only God had beaten him in the end.

This is one of several crucial passages in *Sunset Song* where Mitchell is clearly coming to terms with his own family, background and culture, seeing with new eyes the pattern of their life. And yet the wounding ambivalence about the realities of this life is ever-present. In some moods Mitchell might have said of the Mearns what Lawrence said of Sicily: "It is so clear, so beautiful, like the physical beauty of the Greeks. Yet the lives of the people all seem so squalid, so pottering, so despicable: like a crawling of beetles. And then the moment you get outside the grey and squalid walls of the village, how wonderful in the sun, with the land lying apart".

Despite this ambivalence and the tensions within the Guthrie family, there is humour everywhere in the book. The technique by which Mitchell presents this complex texture of darkness and laughter is one of the strengths of his language, a language in which the author's voice is merged with that of the community itself. He is sometimes the omniscient narrator, detached and objective, but more often he is playing a part, a character watching and interpreting the action. In *Sunset Song* the only mind he is ever inside, is that of Chris herself, while all other people's feelings and reactions are registered from the outside: standard English would have been quite inadequate to render this imaginative experience.

For the first half of *Sunset Song* there is no central plot, only a flow of incidents shaping Chris's development. Through all the stages of her growth, her marriage and motherhood, there is still the questioning mind, her sense of the impermanence of life, the search for certainty. As with the short stories 'Clay', 'Sim', and 'Greenden', a sense of apprehension marches alongside the narrative. This becomes focused on the Great War, when destructive forces from the outside break in upon the farming community. The narrative quickens and becomes more concentrated, and the book darkens. The importance of the war for Mitchell can be gauged from the fact that he adds his own name, in the form of James Leslie, to the list of those killed. This is another symbolic death, this time that of his own childhood, which ended in his perception of civilisation's brutal and corrupting powers. And indeed the war was really a personal symbol for the end of Mitchell's life in that community, rather than the end of the community itself. There is no objective evidence that crofting was destroyed by the war, indeed the war years were a boom time for farmers large and small. The forces which undermined crofting were well established before the war, and its decline was a process which was still far from complete even at Mitchell's death.

The imprint of Mitchell's diffusionist and socialist ideas is clearly visible in *A Scots Quair* in the recurring motifs of innocence and corruption. Yet the book's strength is precisely that these themes are not presented in a simplistic or doctrinaire fashion; they are worked out through the human drama, and although these themes are ever-present, no clear or final answers are found. The work is not forced to take the form of a simplistic diffusionist parable since, from the outset in *Sunset Song*, corrupting forces are already present within the Guthrie family and in Kinraddie at large. Chris must first achieve her freedom from this tyranny before her process of self-discovery can move forward. She then experiences a brief period of joy and fulfilment in her marriage. In this central part of *Sunset Song* we are conscious of a wholeness, an innocence, and an equilibrium which is the gift that the rural world should ideally contain. But such peace and equilibrium can be at best temporary in this world; outside forces or inner conflicts will destroy it. This wholeness is lost, found briefly, then lost again during the rest of the *Quair*. The book's deeper theme

"Gulls there were everywhere, Chris was deafened in the clamour of the brutes."

is a meditation on human ambition and endeavour, on the tension between permanence and change, and the inability of all human systems and creeds to achieve this wholeness in the face of change, striving, uncertainty and suffering.

In *Cloud Howe* Chris rebuilds her life with Robert, but this time it is his religion which destroys their relationship. Chris's failed marriage to the kirk's man is unmistakably a symbol of Mitchell's lifelong fascination with religion: he was the thirteenth disciple, seeking a creed but unable to accept the Christian one. The figure of Robert Colquohoun, the humane, rational Christian socialist, is one of the most revealing Mitchell ever drew. It shows how close his beliefs about civilisation and human destiny were to being a religion. D. H. Lawrence was similarly drawn to a secularised religion, and he wrote of St. John's "passionate and mystic hatred of the civilisation of his day, a hatred so intense only because he knew that the living realities of men's being were displaced by it...something to which the soul answers now." But while Mitchell and Lawrence could accept some of the insights of religion, neither could accept its objective truth. Robert's socialism fails him, and he withdraws into mysticism.

In *Cloud Howe* the strong aesthetic and intellectual structure of the trilogy reveals itself more and more clearly. If *Sunset Song* is dominated by the element of the sunlit earth, in *Cloud Howe* it is that of cloud, symbolising Robert's religious and social aspirations, the illusory creed which he believes capable of regenerating the world. In *Grey Granite* the cloud has become the fog of the city in which human dignity and freedom are lost. These underlying themes appear and re-appear like musical motifs, giving a living structure to the work. In *Cloud Howe* the four chapters progress from fair-weather cloud to storm cloud, as Chris's life moves from her healing second marriage to a new and even deeper crisis. Her divided personality is still more pronounced as she finds herself living a life she cannot believe in, spiritually divided from her husband. The intellectual and social conflicts in the real world of the 1920s enter more insistently into her life, determining the course of the narrative and changing her relationship with Robert. The town setting is mirrored in the density of the writing: the texture of events and characters is faster and more varied, and the human comedy is still broader than in *Sunset Song*. Yet like the first part of the trilogy, *Cloud Howe* becomes increasingly dark as it progresses, and the death of Chris's child re-enacts the Mitchell's own tragedy of 1926. Robert's final sermon at the close of the book in an eloquent and despairing epitaph on human aspirations and progress. In the portrait of Ewan as a child, we are once again reminded that Mitchell had no childhood in the modern sense. Cool, humourless, English-speaking, self-reliant, different from all the other children, he embodies all the intellectual aspects of Mitchell's own personality. His character is the cold stone from which a new type of humanity might be fashioned – but at a price. Are we to understand Ewan as an incomplete, even a maimed, personality, or as the inheritor of a primitive nobility that is beyond human weakness and passion? His development comes to have equal weight with Chris's own in *Grey Granite*.

Grey Granite has often been criticised as the least satisfactory part of the *Quair*, and the reason that suggests itself is that Mitchell was dealing here with aspects of life of which he had little personal experience. There is some truth in this, for the book revives something of the brutality and intellectualisation of his English novels and Ewan's development is recognisably in the mould of John Garland and Malcom Maudslay, although his personality is very different from theirs. The Duncairn of the novel is plainly based not on Mitchell's childhood, but on his period as a young man in Aberdeen and Glasgow. Yet the themes and the character of *Grey Granite* are artistically necessary for Mitchell to complete the architecture of the *Quair*. He achieves this by interpreting the Scottish industrial city in the light of his historical and political theories. The harshness and squalor of the city of Duncairn fulfil Mitchell's vision of humanity's historical fall from innocence into twentieth-century chaos. A fragmented, kaleidoscopic technique is used to represent the pace of urban life – different voices, different languages, different environments. The split between Chris and her son is now almost total, and their lives move in irreconcilable directions, he towards political action, she increasingly convinced of the futility of human ambitions. In her mind the motif of *vanitas* grows ever stronger: the obsession with impermanence, and the recurring vision of death waiting behind all human endeavour. In the divergence between Ewan's overmastering creed and Chris's increasingly bleak life, Mitchell is presenting the enduring conflict between action and passivity, intellect and intuition, commitment and detachment, belief and existential despair. Moreover there are religious echoes again in this win focus on mother and son. Ewan's belief in himself as the instrument of historical change is almost a belief in a secular incarnation: he loses his human identity as he assumes the role of leader. But Chris is locked out from this sense of destiny, mystified by her own son, and their Last Supper together is a bleak leave-taking.

Yet even in *Grey Granite* we have not left entirely the world of Mitchell's childhood, for it is during the various excursions from the city into the surrounding countryside that the most significant personal experiences take place. We perceive that however different each part of the *Quair* may be, each is necessary to express Mitchell's vision. It is interwoven of experience and intellect, but the personal and geographical setting holds the two in successful balance. The *Quair* is more than the poetry of *Sunset Song*: each of its parts modifies and illuminates the other, so that Mitchell's vision of man's progress from the country to the city, from innocence to corruption, is fully realised in this book as in none of his others. And deeper even than that theme is the more personal one of the conflict between action and despair, the struggle against the destructive forces of time and change.

In the dramatisation of this conflict. *A Scots Quair* is strikingly anti-intellectual: again and again human achievements and human philosophies are questioned, mocked, or dismissed as powerless in the face of time and change. This instinctive pessimism is very different from the doctrinal certainty of Mitchell's English books, and it shows how far he had matured as a writer. Writers and philosophers of the 1920s, the post-war wasteland, were drawn to many different creeds and systems, from Wells' utopian socialism to Lawrence's sexual mysticism. Mitchell had clearly been part of this process, and his entire literary output testified to the strength of his belief in his own view of history and human civilisation. Yet as the *Quair* progresses into an ever darker and bleaker world, he has the integrity to question the very possibiity of any form of human regeneration, either social or personal.

Ultimately we do not know where his own belief finally rested, whether in the creed as clear and sharp as a knife, or in the poet's intuition of the devouring darkness. This is partly a feminine disillusionment with men's philosophies and men's use of power: the feminine persona derived from Ray is of enormous value here as a counterbalance to Mitchell's tendency to over-intellectualisation. Here Mitchell was inspired to abandon clear-cut answers, to follow his instinct, and leave the enigma unresolved. Ewan sets off to find a new future, while Chris returns to the place of her birth, imagining not merely that there is no future, but that there has been no past, that her life might have been a mere play of shadows, leaving the questions all unanswered. Mitchell had elements of both these people within him. He had Ewan's idealism but not his single-mindedness, and he never engaged in active politics after his brief experience in Glasgow. But he did not go back to live in rural Scotland either: he could not, because Scotland was his childhood, and he sensed the impossibility of returning to the past. After his death his widow's first desire was to move with her children back to a small farm somewhere in the North-East. She eventually decided against this, but her impulse suggests that she, like Chris, was tempted to turn back the clock, and to inhabit again the world that Mitchell had portrayed.

Mitchell's legacy has been powerful and enduring. His work is a literary classic, but more important it has entered the popular consciousness of Scotland. But beyond the obvious one of its setting, does it have an inner Scottish dimension? Mitchell had a great scorn for the familiar emblems of Scottish nationhood – the castles, the kirk, the Stewarts, the cult of Burns. He regarded them as mere symbols, opiates to distract attention from the realities of history. But in this, Scottish culture was no different from other cultures: all history was written and all high culture defined by the lairds and clerics, the rulers and scholars who shaped the destiny of nations, or wrote the annals of the parish from the top looking downwards. Ewan's contemptuous dismissal of classical art and music ("You looked away and about the room, flat seascapes and landscapes, the deadest stuff, why did people make a fuss of pictures. Or Music? You'd never seen anything in either?") was Mitchell himself speaking. This distrust of culture as an illusion, merely a distracting game, lay behind his antipathy to Scottish Nationalism: he could not believe that a revival of Scots identity in politics or literature or language was an aim worth striving for. Seen in the perspective of twentieth-century chaos, it would achieve nothing for the vast majority of Scottish people. On the contrary he sought the dissolution of nations, barriers and false identities based on empty symbols. All this he believed with his intellect, and yet he was keenly aware of the fundamental dichotomy in the Scottish psyche, the lack of wholeness: Scotland was a nation without statehood, a people not in control of its own life, a consciousness fed on symbols. When he wrote his Scottish novel he penetrated beneath those symbols: its Scottish dimension lies in its focus on the crofting tradition of independence, dignity and control over their own lives. The crofters' nobility, skill and endurance reached back to a time before the history of kings and governments, and preserved a dignity that urban life destroyed. This was Scotland to Mitchell, something oblique, unromantic and elusive. In giving expression to this tradition he added a new element not merely to

Scottish literature, but to world literature too, for his work has no real language barrier and is accessible to anyone familiar with peasant communities.

Yet alongside this vision of an essential nobility in the Scots peasant, Mitchell could not resist exposing and ridiculing the malice and meanness of spirit that he felt were also part of the northern inheritance. Like Lawrence once again he felt that "Over these countries, like the grey skies, lies the gloom of the dark moral judgement and condemnation and reserve of the people". The conventional culprit – Scots Calvinism – was to Mitchell merely a localised symptom of the poison of civilisation. This dichotomy between nobility and degeneracy provided Mitchell with ample scope for the pitiless realism in his portrait of Scottish society which so angered many people, both in the Mearns and beyond. The Scots trilogy was widely regarded as a mere satire, a betrayal of the lives and values of local people. This was the aspect of the trilogy that intensified the sense of remoteness that his parents felt towards him. It created a hostility to Mitchell that has only recently faded into the past, as the men and women of his own generation have passed away and his work has become part of history.

The experience of exile in space or time has been a powerful force in twentieth-century literature, and the *Quair* is one of a number of great imaginative reconstructions of a writer's past. It may be that the loss of wholeness felt by the exile makes more urgent the artistic re-creation of that wholeness. Joyce's *Ulysses* was completed two decades after he left Dublin for ever. For Joyce, selfhood was to be constructed by finding intellectual traditions beyond those he had inherited. In this search, expatriation from the narrow world of his birth was essential. It was equally essential for Lawrence, who sought a self uncluttered by history and culture, who was stifled by the rigidities of English life. Lawrence's critique of England and his search for a philosophy of regeneration was deeply influenced by his years in Italy and Mexico; indeed in his perpetual, restless, unsatisfied travels he was seeking some pure, un-European form of life into which he might enter. Nearer to Mitchell's own experience, Edwin Muir's childhood move from his native Orkney to Glasgow set up tensions in his psyche which fed his creativity with its essential life-themes. Mitchell's exile and his use of the symbol of exploration through space and time serve to link him with all these writers. The experience of exile was two-edged: it might diminish the importance of the writer's early life by revealing new environments and new perspectives – this was the experience Mitchell sought when he left the Mearns; but it might also compel a re-evaluation of the basic elements of personality, the sense of place and the sense of inheritance that shape our lives in ways we cannot control. In the case of Muir and Mitchell, the experience of exile became associated with the search for a place or a time beyond the chaos of history. Both writers have a strong impulse towards myth-making, revealing what Muir called the fable beneath the story. Mitchell would clearly not have accepted Muir's identification of the place of his childhood with a kind of Eden; but he did see that community as containing in a pure form the elements of an almost mythic conflict between innocence and corruption. Muir pursued his outward journey away from Scotland into European literature, psychology, and internationalism. One part of Mitchell followed such a course, but his deeper self was drawn back into an explicit recreation of his first world, and into the writing of his, and Ray's, alternative life in contemporary Scotland.

This concern with the psychology of self-discovery was one of several broad points of contact between Mitchell and the other writers of his time. In his search for a route to human regeneration in the post-war wasteland, he is recognisably speaking the language of Eliot or Lawrence. Yet, as any great writer has to be, he was a solitary genius pursuing his own vision. He was dismissive of a whole spectrum of past culture, uninterested in art or music, or even in literary experiment for its own sake. For him, man's life was essentially historical, material, analysable, and not aesthetic or mystical. This rigid intellectualism impoverished his English writings, but in probing the roots of his own life in *A Scots Quair* he rediscovered both the life of the instincts and the means to express it. The poet in him was released at last, for it is in many places a poet's novel, sensitive and intuitive, for all its colloquial vitality.

In 1932 the Aberdeen journalist Cuthbert Graham linked Mitchell's name with those of Hardy and Wessex. Mitchell had indeed admired Hardy's fiction and it may have influenced his decision to write his own regional novel. The impulse of a writer to place his work in a real, identifiable location has two main implications. The first is autobiographical: the writer's own world is chosen because it has uniquely familiar elements from which he can build his drama and his vision. The sharpness of place creates for the reader too a dimension of realism that is missing from an imaginary landscape. Yet the second factor is, paradoxically, one of transcendence: the writer is freed from the need to build an artificial, theatrical stage for his characters to inhabit, and he can discern instead the underlying forces which are shaping their lives. By focusing on a known and well-mapped landscape, Mitchell can analyse the real personal, social, or spiritual conflicts which are in play. As in Hardy, the spirit of the place becomes itself a major character and a major force in the book. As in Hardy too it leads to a view of human life that is somehow both secular and transcendent: the blind impersonal fate about which Hardy wrote so much, becomes in *A Scots Quair* the remorseless movement of time and change. This harsh, indefinable force has a god-like power to shape and disfigure human lives, leaving only the land itself unchanged. The expression of this spirit through the features and places of a real landscape is regionalism at its most profound.

Grey Granite was Mitchell's last completed work, the final pages being drafted in September 1934, on Barmekin Hill, while visiting with Alexander Gray at his home in Echt. Just five months before his death he completed in fictional form the pattern of exile and homecoming which is the most striking aspect of life as a writer. He had begun a new novel of the Mearns, written in the idiom of the *Quair*, and it seems probable that it was to contain directly autobiographical elements, centred on the character of the strange, gifted child Keith Stratoun. But it must be doubted that he could have repeated his achievement in the *Quair*. He had something unique to say and he had said it with skill and with passion. The overwhelming fact about *A Scots Quair* in the context of Mitchell's work is its subjectivity: it was written out of his own life, in a way that he did not consciously control. It demanded to be written in the language of the region and through the people of the region. What, ultimately, was he saying about that society? What drew him to write about this world after an exile of fifteen years? Firstly he had seen other societies, in Glasgow, in London, in the army and in the Middle East. He found them rootless, corrupted, squalid and cruel, and his perspective on the traditional community of the Mearns was inevitably changed by those experiences. But the crucial transformation in his mind was his understanding of the roles people played in a traditional society. In the roles of master and man, priest and people, farmer and crofter he saw a microcosm of human history, that within these roles the individual could reveal his essential nobility, accepting or resisting the powers that confronted him. There was thus an identity between his mature vision of history and his childhood perceptions. In order to confront reality he had only to look into the springs of his own life and its conflicting forces. Only the painful development of his life and mind outside the Mearns had given him the perspective to understand and value what he had left behind. The exact process behind the psychological transformation that created *A Scots Quair* will never be known. But on his visits north each summer between 1925 and 1931,

he came to see that his childhood world contained all the elements
with which to dramatise his perception of good and evil. What he
wrote of had always been there, but he now realised that he had never
seen it. But he achieved his vision, and recaptured the time that he
had lost. He learned what all creative writers must learn in order to
tap the springs of originality, that "What we have not had to
decipher, to elucidate by our own efforts, what was clear before we
looked at it, is not ours".

Sources and Further Reading

The basic reference work for Mitchell's life is IAN MUNRO: *James Leslie Mitchell: Lewis Grassic Gibbon*, 1966. The papers which Munro used were then in Ray Mitchell's possession but are now in the National Library of Scotland, the main sequence of files is MS 26036 – 26103. All the quotations in this book from Mitchell's letters, from Ray's collections, from Alexander Gray, John Mitchell, Hugh MacDiarmid and others are taken from these files. Historical documents such as birth certificates and valuation rolls are of course in the public archives, mainly in Register House, Edinburgh. Smaller collections of Mitchell's papers are to be found elsewhere, such as the Grassic Gibbon Centre in Arbuthnott and Edinburgh University Library. It is unlikely that significant documents relating to Mitchell's life remain to be discovered. Munro's book is long out of print, as is the best study of Mitchell as a writer, DOUGLAS YOUNG: *Beyond the Sunset*, 1973. Still in print at the time of writing is W. K. MALCOLM: *Blasphemer and Reformer*, 1987, a detailed study of Mitchell's philosophical ideas.

I have consulted many other books for the wider background to Mitchell's life. For the historical context see T. C. SMOUT: *A Century of the Scottish People, 1830-1950*, 1986. More specifically, IAN CARTER: *Farm-Life in North-East Scotland: The Poor Man's Country*, 1979 investigates the sociology of the farming community, as do LYNN JAMIESON & CLAIRE TOYNBEE: *Country Bairns: Growing Up 1900-1930*, 1993. EMMA LETLEY: *From Galt to Douglas Brown: Nineteenth Century Fiction and Scots Language*, 1988, describes the Scots language in novels before Mitchell. VALENTINE CUNNINGHAM: *British Writers of the Thirties*, 1988, is full of insights into the literary scene of the period. Two essential books which compress an enormous amount of research are RODERICK WATSON: *The Literature of Scotland*, 1984, and MICHAEL LYNCH: *Scotland: A New History*, 1991. Finally the six inch to one mile Ordnance Survey maps of Kincardineshire and Aberdeenshire from the early years of this century can illuminate many details of Mitchell's background.